LITTLE PLATOONS

LITTLE PLATOONS

HOW A REVIVED ONE NATION CAN EMPOWER ENGLAND'S FORGOTTEN TOWNS AND REDRAW THE POLITICAL MAP

DAVID SKELTON

Biteback Publishing

First published in Great Britain in 2019 by
Biteback Publishing Ltd
Westminster Tower
3 Albert Embankment
London SE1 7SP
Copyright © David Skelton 2019

ISBN 978-1-78590-512-4

10 9 8 7 6 5 4 3 2 1

A CIP catalogue record for this book is available from the British Library.

Set in Adobe Garamond Pro

Printed and bound in Great Britain by
CPI Group (UK) Ltd, Croydon CR0 4YY

CONTENTS

—

'The Durham miners won't wear it.'
HERBERT MORRISON ON THE EUROPEAN COAL
AND STEEL COMMUNITY

'To love the little platoon we belong to in society is the first principle
(the germ as it were) of public affections. It is the first link in the
series by which we proceed towards a love of country and mankind.'
EDMUND BURKE

INTRODUCTION

JUNE 2016 – A REVOLT AGAINST THE STATUS QUO

The vote to leave the EU wasn't just driven by disenchantment with a remote Brussels bureaucracy. It was also a protest against a British political and economic status quo, which had long neglected towns and villages across the country. It was no accident, for example, that of the forty-two former coalfield areas, some forty-one had voted for Brexit.

The shock of the vote meant that, for a time, June 2016 seemed almost like a revolutionary moment in British politics. People in the so-called post-industrial towns had made it quite clear that the economic and political settlement was not working for them and politicians seemed serious about tackling their concerns. Now that seems like a false dawn. The important issues that were highlighted have remained unaddressed and the political and economic settlement remains unchanged.

One of these towns that let out a scream of anger was my home town of Consett, perched high in the north-west corner of County Durham. When the Royal Navy ruled the waves, this was the town that produced its steel and built bridges around the world as a monument to the craft of steelworkers in England's 'far corner'. Workers at the Consett Iron Company took pride in their trade and the people of the town were proud that 'Consett steel' was a symbol of quality around the world.

The story of the referendum and, with it, modern British politics is wrapped up in places like Consett and, as such, my own family history. The concept of why people felt shut out from politics can be explained by what I experienced growing up in a town that came to be known as 'left behind' by both politics and economics following the closure of the steelworks that the town had depended on for over a century. Like many towns, a sense of dignity and security was replaced with one of economic disenchantment and cultural insecurity. Political rhetoric, which came to be dominated by phrases like 'openness' and 'mobility', meant little to people who actually yearned for security and control over their own lives. Even those towns that had escaped the worst ravages of deindustrialisation found themselves facing years of decline as much of their economic life was cut off.

Towns that were once central to the thinking of politicians had become peripheral. Some kept on voting Labour out of habit or family loyalty; few did it out of a sense of enthusiasm or genuine attachment. Plenty of other voters stopped voting altogether as the political settlement seemed less relevant to improving their day-to-day life.

CONCERNS REMAIN UNADDRESSED

For a few fleeting weeks in 2016, following a referendum result that nobody had seen coming (largely because they had stopped listening), people started to talk about these kinds of communities again. Voters in places like Consett voted in numbers that hadn't been seen for decades. The 'left behind' became a vogueish, if nebulous, phrase (somehow implying that people and communities had been left behind accidentally), with the new Tory Prime Minister reaching extraordinary, but brief, heights of popularity while talking about 'burning injustices' and 'an economy that works for everybody'. Journalists were desperate to dedicate column inches to the members of the so-called forgotten Britain – for a while at least.

As mentioned earlier, however, the economic reform hasn't happened yet and the old economic and political settlement remains firmly in place. The media and politicians found something else to preoccupy them and simply moved on. This is something that those who had actually been 'left behind' in places like Consett had no option of doing. Whereas dissatisfaction remains, the political and media debate has become obsessed with the 'horse race' of Brexit and the intricacies of Westminster Village politics. While voters wanted to know how Brexit would impact on their lives, media coverage continued to fascinate on how it would impact the City of London.

The post-referendum period also saw the rise of a socially acceptable snobbery, where the white working class became openly belittled and besmirched. A political and economic class that had ignored and forgotten places like Consett for decades leading up to the referendum seemed inclined again to look the other way and brush the social, economic and political consequences of their actions under the carpet. Once again, there was little inclination rovide a sense of agency and control to people who felt they'd had those powers taken away from them.

Too many seem ready to find excuses to look away and not interact with concerns about the economic and political settlement, particularly in white, working-class communities – with many regarding respect for locality as 'small-mindedness', patriotism as 'xenophobia', and concern about the impact of globalisation as 'bigotry'. The groupthink that condemned working-class people had also produced an elite consensus for the Iraq War, the ERM debacle, a housing crisis and the banking crash – catastrophes that had been created by an elite apparently 'in possession of the facts' and largely opposed by an apparently ignorant populace.

There is an urgent need to deliver the changes that the referendum result demanded. Too many decision-makers, however, still seem quaintly wedded to the laissez-faire liberalism on the right or the top-down socialism on the left that helped create the problem and still seem broadly detached from those communities that had delivered the electoral shock in 2016.

I decided to write this book for a number of reasons. First, the level of snobbery and denigration directed at good people in towns across the country made me genuinely angry. Second, because of the inability of so many to grasp the need for a radical alteration in the political and economic settlement and the fact that widely held views have become unheard in a politics that has failed to challenge old certainties. Third, the belief that the rich tradition of 'One Nation', which helps to unlock many of today's problems, has become lost in a swirl of dogma and it is important to rediscover this tradition.

I remember coming across the speeches of Disraeli and other giants of One Nation several years ago when it seemed that someone growing up in Consett could be either Labour or nothing. It became clear to me then that there was another way between the dogmatism of the free market right and the blinkered nature of the socialist left – both banging the drum for utopian, unrealistic concepts. Whereas the right had stopped believing in community, social justice and society, the left had stopped believing in country, belonging and prosperity. It became clear that One Nation, despite being long forgotten, was uniquely placed to address our societal and economic issues. What was true then is even more so now, as those problems have worsened and divides have deepened.

Boris Johnson has now been elected Prime Minister with a strong message that he wants to deliver the kind of One Nation reforms in the UK as a whole that he did in London (including dramatically spreading the London living wage). He's right to have these big ambitions to create One Nation and deliver substantial domestic reform. In his first speech as Prime Minister, he set out why some of the issues I've addressed in this book should be regarded as a national priority:

> Just a few miles away from here [Manchester] the story is very different. Towns with famous names, proud histories, fine civic buildings where unfortunately the stereotypical story of the last few decades has been long-term decline. Endemic health problems. Generational unemployment. Down-at-heel high streets. The story has been, for young people growing up there, of hopelessness, or the hope that one day they'll get out and never come

back ... And in so far as that story is true, and sometimes it is, the crucial point is it isn't really the fault of the places and it certainly isn't the fault of the people growing up there – they haven't failed. No, it is we, us the politicians, the politics, that has failed.

Time and again they have voted for change, but for too long politicians have failed to deliver on what is needed.

It was important to hear a Prime Minister focus his first major policy speech on places and voters that had long been ignored by politicians of both parties.

In this book, my aim is to help consider the foundations for a renewed economic and political settlement so that it works for someone in Consett as much as it works for somebody in the City of London. This is based on the premise that we have to understand what has gone wrong before we can consider how to put it right.

In Chapter One, I'll discuss my experience of growing up in Consett as it moved from global industrial powerhouse to national symbol of industrial decline, before considering what this has meant in terms of both economic and political disempowerment. Chapter Two will then address how this experience has been shared in forgotten towns across the country, with such towns and villages that have become cut off from many of the benefits of economic growth and ignored by generations of politicians. Here I will consider how policies ranging from the expansion of higher education to poor focus on transport and infrastructure have had a damaging impact on towns across the country. Chapter Three will then consider the millions of voters who do not believe that

their views, backgrounds or concerns have been adequately represented in politics. It addresses the growth of the political disconnect in greater detail and looks at how a cushioned Westminster
was taken so dramatically by surprise by a Brexit vote driven by
long-forgotten towns.

Chapter Four discusses the factors that have played a bigger
role than any other in breaking the social contract between government and the governed. It will consider how a response to
deindustrialisation created a sense of marginalisation that, over
decades, developed into alienation and disengagement. It will
then consider how the biggest wave of mass migration in British history (conducted without prior consent) and the political
response to the banking crash also weakened the social contract
and diminished the sense of agency and control that people felt,
creating a sense that decisions were made *for* people rather than
by them.

This disengagement has partially been caused by the growth
of dogmatic ideologies that fail to offer adequate solutions to the
problems of the day. A myopic economic liberalism or one-eyed,
old-fashioned socialism cannot come close to addressing the
issues we are facing today.

Chapter Five argues that the economic liberalism that has
largely held sway over recent decades has made some important
changes, but, in some cases, it has hardened into a dogma, while
failing to deliver the popular share and property ownership or the
broadened prosperity that many had promised. I argue that the
centre-right needs to embrace a more nuanced approach to the
role of the state in order to empower people economically and

politically and to create conditions in which entrepreneurialism can flourish.

The companion to this economic liberalism has been a relentless growth of identity liberalism, which has become shallow and all-embracing. Chapter Six considers how this identity liberalism has also seen the white working class reduced to the bottom of the list and has sought to diminish unifying narratives. Both economic and identity liberalism have made society more atomised, have reduced feelings of solidarity and cohesion and resulted in social issues such as loneliness, alienation and a diminished sense of community.

Chapter Seven talks about how the emotional connection between the Labour Party and working-class towns has diminished, as the growth of identity liberalism has coincided with the party becoming more bourgeois in membership, policy priorities and voter base. Such a shift has left it out of sympathy and out of step with the voters in England's 'forgotten towns' who once provided the party's emotional core. This offers an opening for a fundamental realignment of politics for a party that develops a renewed political and economic settlement.

Proposed solutions such as turbo-charged economic liberalism or a reversion to old-style socialism show little imagination and risk entrenching existing inequalities or making the problems worse. It's hard to see how a reheated socialism that has failed many times before would work any better today. Similarly, a solution driven from the centre would do nothing to restore a sense of national or local community. We shouldn't pretend that society must face a choice between doctrinaire, reductionist economic liberalism on the one hand and doctrinaire and reductionist old-style socialism on the other. Life is more complicated than that and our approach to public policy should be more nuanced. Boris Johnson's full-throated endorsement of higher infrastructure spending and a higher living wage shows that he's happy to reject the doctrinaire in favour of the policies the country needs.

In Chapter Eight, I argue that a rediscovery of One Nation ideas, which have become obscured by economic liberalism, could provide the basis for the new economic and political settlement that people are craving. It could also provide a political vehicle to redraw the political map. This chapter sets out how One Nation, with its belief in national unity, private enterprise and intelligent use of the state, could help to address the central issues that have led to the current sense of political and economic crisis. I'll seek to re-evaluate the One Nation tradition and explain why it is more relevant than ever today – helping to extricate the country from a situation where the two nations that Disraeli warned about are dangerously close to being a reality.

Finally, Chapter Nine will outline the basis for a renewed settlement based on One Nation principles. It will argue that refining our politics and economics in a way that promotes unity rather than division must become a priority. It's no longer good enough to accompany rhetoric about the 'left behind' with little or no action. Our politics needs to be genuinely progressive and patriotic. It also needs to be populist in the best sense of the word – that politics should be run in the interests of the great mass of people, rather than powerful vested interests. This politics needs to be based around the nation state, rather than transnational institutions that are too distant and aren't able to capture loyalty from the bulk of voters or a sense of social solidarity needed to build and maintain social institutions.

The process of Brexit provides us with an opportunity to consider what kind of country we want to be and how we can reunify after the divisions caused by the referendum and its aftermath. Plenty of people in Consett and elsewhere voted 'Leave' because of a desire to 'Take Back Control'. In the concluding chapter, I'll consider how people lost their sense of control, agency and security and how this can be regained. My goal is to set out an agenda that would genuinely give back control to people who have lost it in recent decades and create a sense of empowerment and engagement in disempowered towns.

I recommend a massive programme of national reconstruction with a focus on providing infrastructure to those towns that have been 'left behind'. This will be accompanied by a sweeping phase of devolution, allowing local areas to innovate to become economically vibrant again and actively engaging local people in this process, accompanied by policies that are both pro-business and pro-worker. It would look to recreate the entrepreneurial zeal in those towns that once drove Britain to industrial greatness, utilising incentives for business investment and growth.

The agenda I set out puts an emphasis on skill and vocation, making sure that struggling towns have the skills to put them at the forefront of emerging industrial revolutions. It would work with businesses to ensure that major vocational institutions are based in areas that need them the most and would push to ensure that the best schools, with the best teachers, are in those towns that need them the most. These proposals would look to directly empower workers, through home ownership, share ownership and greater engagement in the way in which their companies are run. They seek to help create a dynamic, job-creating economy that benefits everybody, but also strengthen families and communities.

It's an important, but secondary, consideration that the One Nation agenda I set out will not only improve people's lives in long-forgotten communities, but could also reshape British politics. Traditional party loyalties are diminishing, and this agenda would enable a shrewd Tory Party to build a new and lasting electoral coalition. It is a positive agenda that could be socially, economically and politically transformative.

I decided to call this book *Little Platoons* as that old Edmund Burke phrase encapsulates the importance of family, community and place. These 'little platoons' should be more important than ever in a society that has become fractured by a growing sense of atomisation and alienation and a politics that has stopped delivering for millions of Britons.

Fundamentally, the agenda set out in the pages that follow is a positive one, seeking to create One Nation again. I believe that this country is the best country in the world and that our best days lie ahead of us. I hope that this book makes a tiny contribution to carving an agenda of political renewal and national reconstruction in which all citizens feel that they can play a significant and active part.

CHAPTER ONE

WORK THAT YOU CAN BE PROUD OF

The waters of the river Derwent are, it is said, of a peculiar soft-ness, particularly well-suited to steelmaking. The Derwent is the river running through the vicinity of Consett in the northern part of County Durham. The softness of the water encouraged a handful of German families, the Oleys and Moles, to settle in the nearby village of Shotley Bridge in 1691.

This started a long tradition of steelmaking in the Consett area that was to last for almost three centuries. The German settlers quickly became famous for the particular quality of their swords and cutlery. On one occasion, William Oley took up a challenge with other steelmakers to make the most resilient sword. Oley turned up to the challenge not visibly carrying a sword, leading the others to think that he had forfeited the challenge. Instead, Oley removed his top hat and showed the other swordmakers a sword coiled within his hat, which they could only remove with a vice. He not only won the challenge but also illustrated that swordmaking in the Consett area was technologically ahead of the rest of England. Later, with the Napoleonic Wars, Consett became cemented as a global centre for swordmaking. The razor firm Wilkinson Sword emerged from this early industry, and the local pub is still called the 'Crown And Crossed Swords'.

The tale of the Oleys and the Moles is symbolic of what Consett and its steelworks came to represent to local people. There was real pride in highly skilled work and a trade that made this small, snowy town a genuine global leader. Workers for these German settlers were also paid and treated well. They laid the foundations for a golden age of steel that would last until well into the twentieth century, until Consett became one of the first industry towns to lose the industry that it depended on.

In the early years of the nineteenth century, Jonathan Richardson and his family would look to take advantage of the waters around Shotley Bridge to turn the village into a spa town – the Harrogate of the north. That didn't go to plan, but the special nature of the water also encouraged the Richardsons to investigate combining the known skills in the area and the special nature of the water to develop steel on a more industrial level. From this arose the steelworks and the Consett Iron Company (known locally merely as 'The Company'). It would gradually rise to become an industrial giant, which dominated the north-eastern economy and contributed enormously to the economy of Britain and the whole Empire. For the next century and a half, steel would define Consett and its people – a steeltown, which produced steelworkers. In the 1980s, this steeltown faced the challenge of what it could be when the steel was taken away.

It's hard to imagine what it would have been like to have lived through the golden age of steel in Consett. Many people still talk about it as though it were yesterday, even though any kind of golden age is now rapidly disappearing from living memory. This small outpost in north-west Durham came to be one of the biggest suppliers of steel in the world. If the British Empire was made on the playing fields of Eton, then the steel that built its structures and its battleships was made in the streets of Consett. And the coal that powered its industry and its expansion came from the surrounding pit villages.

Consett steelworks produced the steel for some of the foremost achievements of Britain and its Empire. Blackpool Tower and bridges around the world still stand as landmarks to the steel the town produced. For years, Roker Park played a similar role, as well as a number of the frigates and warships that helped Britannia rule the waves, and the nuclear submarines of the post-war period. The steelworks also played an important role in the social and sporting life of nearby communities. Consett cricket and football clubs were both built by the steelworks, and nearby social clubs also had close connections to the steel plant. The steelworks was home to world-leading engineers, metallurgists and chemists and dozens of different types of craftsmen who passed these skills on to apprentices.

As one of the historians of the steelworks observed:

> There can be no doubt that Consett had a highly skilled and justifiably proud workforce with an international reputation for the specialised steels they produced ... Almost every worker expressed pride in the part they played at the Works, and rightly so. The labourers as well as the skilled men could look to the quality of the product they created. They could look to the history and tradition of the Works, the tradition of their fathers, their grandfathers and their great grandfathers who had worked in the same plant for

over a century. They were proud of the sheer hard graft that they put into an incredibly heavy industry, at times harder than any other. It is now fashionable to denigrate the idea of 'men's work', but that phrase accurately described the sweat, heat, dirt and acute danger involved at places like the blast or the coke works. They could look to the sheer size of the operation and the part they played in making this industrial monster work. The steelworkers have every right to look back on what they did, what they built and what their fathers built, with a sense of satisfaction. It is unlikely ever to be forgotten.

The town was also surrounded by the pits of the famous Durham and Northumberland coalfields. To this day, this heritage is still celebrated at the Durham Miners' Gala, where villagers continue to march, from the early morning of the first Saturday in July, from villages scattered around County Durham past the County Hotel in Durham towards the city's cathedral and former racecourse. The shipyards at Swanhunter in Newcastle and in nearby Sunderland were also supplied with Consett steel. Steelworking, and, in particular, mining, was a dangerous occupation that bred community spirit and strong feelings of solidarity. Communities tended to be places where, because of this sense of danger, people looked out for each other.

The people who worked in the steelmills and coal mines were respected, too, and even shown a degree of reverence by politicians of both left and right. Herbert Morrison famously, and correctly, surmised that 'the Durham miners won't wear it' when presented with plans to create a European Coal and Steel Community (the embryonic European Union). Later, but expressing feelings that he articulated all of his adult life, Harold Macmillan talked about miners as 'the best men in the world ... the men who beat the Kaiser's army and beat Hitler's army ... and never give in.'

In recent decades, the national focus has drifted away from places like Consett – once at the centre of the national conversation, now barely at the periphery. Political attention focused on things that meant little or nothing to voters in the Derwent Valley – the 'benefits' of EU membership, seemingly symbolised by structural funding that hadn't made any difference to people's day-to-day lives, and obsession with statistics such as GDP, where political boasts didn't seem to reflect the situation on the ground.

RISE AND DECLINE

I was born steeped in this heritage and this tradition. My grandad on my dad's side was a foreman fitter in the Consett steelworks, or 'the works' as everybody in the town knew it, when they were at their post-war peak. Several other members of his family also followed him into work there. My mother's dad was a miner (or 'pitman' as they preferred to be called) in the Durham and Northumberland coalfields. He and my grandmother had two religions – socialism and methodism, each of which arguably fed into the other, and were a large part of life in the villages of Low Westwood and Chopwell, where my mother grew up.

The other side of industrial life was summed up by the fact that both my grandads died in their early sixties from factors related to their workplaces. My pitman grandad died of pneumoconiosis – a grim disease, known as 'black lung', caused by coal dust building up on the lungs for a prolonged period, leading to eventual lung failure. The nature of mining meant that this disease was generally suffered by coal miners, so it was little wonder that he didn't want anyone else in his family to 'work in a hole in the ground'.

This is a reminder that the 'glory years' of Consett and the Durham coalfield were characterised by back-breaking and difficult work. Some of this gets lost in the romanticisation of industrial working-class life in modern discourse, often by the urban middle class. The early years of Consett were rife with race riots, between locals and the large contingent of Irish immigrants who came to fill the rising number of jobs created by the steelworks and their surrounding industries. Indeed, some of the worst 'race riots' in the country occurred during the 1840s in Consett. During this period of violence, the town only had two policemen, making it a place of some lawlessness.

To quote Kearney again:

> Consett was a violent society from the start. It was brutal and brutalising ... Isolation was so complete that it held people together and it gave them the strength and the humour to endure the dirt and the discord, the unending miseries and pressures. The Company took a desolate moorland and created an entire town ... The town the Company built did not conquer the howling wilderness, the town the Company built contained the howling wilderness.

Despite growing from a small hamlet to a town of around 10,000 by the end of the Victorian era, for much of the period of growth, the town had little to no basic facilities. Consett experienced a growth surge in the early to mid-nineteenth century, but it wasn't until 1860 that the town had piped water. Nearby Stanley didn't have water until ten years later. Consett was, for much of its early years, a town that had 'more beer than water'. The town's historian, Tony Kearney, says that Consett was basically a 'workcamp' until the early years of the twentieth century, when it started to illustrate the hallmarks of a town. No hospital was built until 1870 and there was no infirmary until 1879. The death rate was appallingly high; in one year in Leadgate some eighty-one people died, contrasted with the one hundred from the same village who were killed during the entirety of the First World War. Forty-three of these eighty-one deaths were children under five years old, illustrating quite how poor the sanitary conditions were. Work accidents were frequent, as were deaths resulting from these accidents.

The 'company slums' were gradually replaced by surrounding housing estates designed by the Company to serve the Company's needs. Delves Lane, The Grove and The Dene were built in the 1920s. Moorside (which contained the school attended by steelworkers' children from the 1960s onwards) was built in the 1930s. Within the limits of the time (Consett was no Bournville; the Iron Company owners were not north-eastern equivalents of Robert Owen), the Iron Company was relatively paternalist and helped provide many of the institutions that served the community well. This included gradually improved housing and schools, but also working men's and social clubs, sporting facilities (the cricket and football clubs still bear the hallmark of the Consett Iron Company). As Kearney and others have pointed out, the industrialists didn't leave the legacy of the likes of the Chamberlains in

Birmingham – there were no statues, grand town halls, beautiful gardens, art galleries or concert halls. The Iron Company might not have been a model employer, but it did at least understand that intermediary institutions help to bind communities.

The Company also realised the importance of engaging workers in the running of the firm, to at least some extent. Indeed, it was only when the steelworks were nationalised that decisions about the works started to be taken hundreds of miles away from Consett itself. Nationalisation was only one of several reasons for Consett's decline, but it was a reason. Politicians were less inclined to lose sleep about the loss of jobs in what they saw as a distant region, which operated as an effective one-party state. Nationalisation resulted in overall management being less engaged in the community, and decisions being made hundreds of miles from the steelworks themselves, often meaning that investment in much-needed modernisation fell victim to a desire for public spending cuts and left the company exposed to a swing in national politics.

Even though conditions obviously improved through the ages, the work was still dangerous, particularly in the nearby mines. Even after measures to improve health and safety, a lifetime of work inhaling coal dust took the life of many men (including, as I've mentioned, my grandad) far too early, and a lifetime of work underground left many others with breathing difficulties and unshakeable injuries. For many, the closure of the pits itself wasn't a source of mourning; rather, it was the loss of community spirit and the fact that nothing remotely equivalent was found to replace them.

The dangers of the job were combined with a clear and visible sign of the environmental damage caused by some of the work being done at the steelworks and some of the health risks to local people. Relatives talk to me about the red snow that fell in the freezing Consett winter. Even that red dust is remembered fondly, with a local brewery naming its celebrated beer after it.

The 'red dust' that is symbolic of Consett was, of course, pollution. A memory that friends and family recall is of the dust covering washing lines, cars and houses, leaving a lingering redness even after the steelworks had closed. This 'dust' didn't just provide an aesthetic glean, it also got in people's eyes, in their lungs and on their skin. Surveys in the 1970s named Consett the dirtiest town in the country, and a survey by Durham University found that residents of local villages were 300 times more likely to get food poisoning than the rest of the country. This pollution was actually avoidable. Fans had been installed to prevent the red dust, but they were regarded as too expensive to use on a regular basis.

As the *Consett Guardian* reported in the 1970s,

> Cars from Consett are easily identifiable. They wear a permanent coat of rusty red, and often of other noxious substances that do nothing to improve the paintwork. To the industrialists and their wives visiting Consett for the first time, probably already conditioned to the cloth-cap, pit heap image of the North East, the swilling of beer and the whippets, Consett must be the last straw.

An important incident in the late 1850s, at the height of laissez-faire economics, also illustrates a crucial difference between the importance of manufacturing to that so-called golden age and manufacturing during the revival of laissez-faire over a century later. When the founders ran into financial difficulties due to excessive speculation and the collapse of a local bank, the Bank of England stepped in to pay the wages until the ownership of the company could be settled. The fact that London authorities recognised the social and economic importance to the broader economy of the manufacturing of steel made a stark contrast to the situation a hundred years later.

AFTER THE WORKS HAD GONE

The furnaces that had made my home town relatively prosperous and its workers relatively secure were turned off in 1980. For many it was as though the world had stopped, and economically, for several, it might as well have done. Consett steel was, according to decision-makers in London, no longer competitive on world markets. Its wages were too high, its furnaces out of date. Neither national unions nor the national Labour Party were seen as putting up much of a fight.

The fact that, three decades later, western Europe is still able to produce steel that is competitive on the world market continues to rankle. While manufacturing as a share of GDP is as low as 10 per cent in the UK, it's still 20 per cent in Germany and almost 30 per cent in South Korea. The UK has deindustrialised more than any other G20 country, and its lagging productivity levels are to a large extent down to a relative lack of high productivity manufacturing.

When the last furnace fell silent, the impact on the town and the surrounding area was devastating. For a time, Consett had the highest rate of unemployment in Europe as a huge proportion of the town's male workforce were told that they were surplus to requirements. As the *Northern Echo* recalled, 'On that afternoon of 12 September 1980, Consett became the first one-industry town to lose the very source of what had brought it to life. The first of a grim cull of major industrial closures that would throw millions on the dole.'

Ellen Wilkinson, the local MP at the time of the Jarrow Crusade, famously described Jarrow in the 1920s and 1930s as the 'town that was murdered'. Consett wasn't murdered in the 1980s, but it felt that way to many when the town lost the industry it relied upon and was faced with cold dispassion from the government and technocrats who made the decision.

As the Rt Rev. David Jenkins, then Bishop of Durham, wrote around a decade after the steelworks had closed: 'Consett came to be right where it is on the exposed moors which are nowhere near anywhere in particular because of the Iron and Steelworks ... So Consett is still where it is without the reason why it came to be where it is.'

Three and a half thousand jobs went with the closure of the works, followed by almost 3,000 more in the supply chain. A year later, male unemployment was a third of the workforce and over 80 per cent of young people were either out of work or on a training scheme. Government retraining was inferior to that offered to victims of such economic catastrophes in places like Germany, with its employment plans and vocationally focused retraining. The fact that nobody had money to spend also led to the closing down of shops in the town.

Men who had defined themselves by their work suddenly found that there was no work around. If people did find new jobs, it was generally the case that their work didn't have anything like the pride or prestige that went with being an employee of the Iron Company. Secure jobs were replaced with insecure ones and the cultural cohesion of the town diminished. Steel was what had given Consett its meaning, and work was what provided meaning, both within the town and within the family structure, to many of the men who lived there.

Social problems followed in the wake of its closure. Previously having a job was seen as a central part of masculinity. After the closure, with half or more of the men in some streets out of work, having a job was no longer the norm, and many reached retirement age without ever having the opportunity to work again.

GROWING UP IN THE SHADOW
OF THE STEELWORKS CLOSURE

I was born in the late 1970s, when the future of this industrial giant was already under threat. I didn't get to meet my grandad on my dad's side, who'd been an engineer in the steelworks. His eldest son worked there too. Nor did I get to meet my mum's father – the only memories I have of him are multiple stories and family portraits where the half-smoked cigarette in hand was ever present.

My grandmothers were both northern matriarchs in their own ways. My maternal grandmother stood by her two religions of methodism and socialism until she died in the house the family had bought from the Coal Board – still convinced that one of those promised lands was just around the corner. My grandma on my dad's side might have stood at only four or so feet, but I saw her strike terror into hardy ex-steelworkers. She always reminded me of the importance of family and community. Until she died in her late nineties, all five of her children, plus dozens of grandkids and great-grandchildren (and plenty of dogs too), would gather in her small bungalow on Christmas Day. The portraits, mugs and tea towels of monarchs from Victoria to Elizabeth were a constant reminder of a very real working-class patriotism.

People gave Consett one of those clunky names that most people never use. They deemed it a 'mono-industrial town', meaning that it was a town that relied for its employment largely on one industry. The fact that most men in the town worked either in the steelworks or in the supporting industries created a real sense of identity, but also left the town badly exposed when the oxygen was cut off from the industry it relied upon. Then it was given another clunky name – that of a 'post-industrial town'.

My dad was one of the lucky ones. He'd been persuaded by his brother not to leave school at the age of fourteen and to pursue his talent for art. He became a teacher in a nearby comprehensive, meaning that our family was guarded from the most severe economic impact of the steelwork closures. My mum worked as a secretary for the police and then for one of the businesses that sprouted up and then disappeared after the steelworks shut down. My dad's painting of Consett steelworks at its peak became one of his bestsellers when he set up as a full-time artist after retiring from teaching – the 'works' might be gone, but they continue to exert a strong emotional hold on the area.

My school life was very much in the shadow of the closure of the steelworks, too. As Consett had one of the highest unemployment rates in Europe in the 1980s, so the deprivations that accompanied this added to the tricky task in school. Moorside Comprehensive had a cricket and football pitch that overlooked what was the site of the works, but had now become a brownfield wasteland. The majority of my fellow pupils claimed free school meals, with their families having been unable to get back into work following the steelworks closure. My schoolfriends had parents who'd been on the dole since the steelworks closed.

There were some great teachers at the school, and I was also lucky to attend an excellent local primary school, but these educators were facing an uphill task. In many ways, the school had to play a role that nobody should have expected it to – picking up the pieces of the social and economic cataclysm that came with the closure of the steelworks. It's probably little surprise that educational performance suffered – the school was ranked one of the worst in County Durham for every year in which I was there and didn't get close to the level of investment in facilities that was needed (lessons were often held in temporary prefabs). There was little talk of university or aspiration; for many in the town, life had been reduced to getting through the week. That is not, of course, to suggest that economic factors should be an excuse for poor educational performance. Indeed, in many ways, delivering the best possible quality of education is even more important in such times. But it would be folly to ignore the inevitable social impact of an economic earthquake.

The school frequently came bottom of a variety of league tables and was often condemned as 'failing'. Looking back, I saw there people who were brighter and smarter than many of the 'high fliers' I see in London now but who were failed by a system that all too easily forgets people like them.

New businesses were popping up, of course, the most famous one being 'Phileas Fogg', a producer of slightly exotic crisps and savoury snacks. The 'Consett airport' adverts of the crisp-makers made the town famous for something other than being home to one of the biggest former steelworks in Europe. Phileas Fogg was bought by KP snacks, who went on to close the factory in 2015. Some former steelworkers also used their redundancy money to build successful businesses. Redundancy payments only went to steelworkers themselves, however, not to the thousands who provided the support jobs that kept the steelworks functioning.

Despite some success stories, nothing came close to offering Consett what the steelworks had – skilled employment that people could be proud of.

For some, the emotional shock of the steelworks closure meant that they didn't work again. The impact on the vibrancy and potential of the town was clear. This wasn't just reflected in unemployment figures, which were as high as 40 per cent in some parts of the area (28 per cent in Consett as a whole), but also by a stark decline in population. By 1990, it had fallen by some 20,000, from 105,000 to 85,000. Plenty of people, especially the young, saw no reason to hang around. The expansion of universities at the same time as the decline in industry meant that towns like Consett were often robbed of the young people who might have helped to turn it around.

Community spirit remained strong. Although people had seen all certainty and security removed, the people in the town made clear that they would get through the worst together. There remained, and still remains, a real sense of pride in what the steelworks had represented and how much a small town in the far corner of England had achieved.

What happened immediately after the closure remains a source of controversy. Large-scale promises of retraining and investment were made in an attempt to cushion the blow, but it's pretty clear that these promises weren't kept.

That this happened at the same time as a so-called economic miracle stuck in the craw of many local people. The '80s and '90s certainly didn't seem very miraculous in Consett. Part of the issue facing politics today is that many of those who have been in power for recent decades think that boom time for them meant boom time for other people.

FORTY YEARS ON

Consett is one of the highest towns in Britain and also, reputably, the snowiest town in England. It is perched in the north-west corner of County Durham, surrounded by the exquisite countryside of both County Durham and Northumberland. This beauty is certainly clearer now than when the furnaces were pumping out smoke four decades ago. It has also attracted many people to live in the local area.

In contrast to the beauty of its surroundings, its town centre is still pockmarked by a collection of charity shops, bargain stores (including Consett's enormous 'Barry's Bargain Store', which has taken over the whole of the old indoor market), travel agents and bookmakers. Although the likes of McDonald's and Starbucks have popped up on the outskirts of the town in recent years and the council's 'Genesis Project' has had some important successes, talk often goes back to what the town once was and the might its steel used to represent.

Much has changed in Consett in the almost forty years since the steelworks closed, but much of the mindset and the anger that accompanied the closure of the works remains the same. The brownfields over which my school looked out on to are now full of new-build homes, increasingly housing people who head off to work in nearby Newcastle or Durham, with Consett taking on many of the characteristics of a dormitory town.

It would be a mistake to cast Consett as some kind of post-industrial dystopia. The population crashed in the years following the steelworks closure, but has since recovered as new housing estates have taken advantage of the proximity to Newcastle and Durham and the stunning north-eastern countryside. Unemployment is also lower than in other parts of the region. These new jobs, however, are predominantly not in Consett. A town that once existed because of its own industry now risks existing as a north-eastern commuter village.

Even my old school seems to have turned the corner. From being described as a failing school when I was there, with only 12 per cent of Year 11 pupils gaining five or more GCSEs at grades A*–C, the school was marked out as one of Tony Blair's transformation academies and saw that figure increase to 62 per cent by 2010. Oddly, this successful model was then merged with another nearby school to form an impersonal super-school, removing the collective memory of the transformation with it.

Despite these improvements, the town is still, in many ways, dominated by low-paid, low-skilled work. Nothing had come close to replacing the steelworks in terms of prestige of work, so many people came to feel that they had 'nothing left to lose' when the vote on membership of the European Union came around in 2016.

The Brexit referendum marked the first time since the 1980s that the national media and politicians started to think about communities like Consett. It became a kind of mantra to talk about the 'left behind', with politicians, economists and commentators falling over themselves to voice their concern. Although they included some of the same politicians, economists and commentators who had advocated and implemented the policies that caused these people to be left behind in the first place, the new level of interest after decades of being ignored wasn't something to be sniffed at. Journalists clambered over themselves to write travelogues of Consett and places like it, often littered with clichés and designed to paste such towns in the worst possible light. Little came of this, however. The discussion continued to be dominated by the interests of the financial services and the City. The 'left behind' were soon abandoned once more.

The fact remains, however, that, in places like Consett, the Brexit vote represented the culmination of decades of discontent with the political and economic establishment. The 1980s saw economic and social devastation, the late 1990s saw renewed hope, followed largely by disappointment, and the twenty-first century was increasingly characterised by alienation and the impact of austerity and recession. The challenge now is to take the message of the Brexit vote and use it to rejuvenate towns around the country that have lacked hope for so long.

CHAPTER TWO

ENGLAND'S FORGOTTEN TOWNS

*Two nations; between whom there is no intercourse and no
sympathy; who are as ignorant of each other's habits, thoughts,
and feelings, as if they were dwellers in different zones,
or inhabitants of different planets.*

– BENJAMIN DISRAELI, *SYBIL*

The referendum on EU membership exposed a clear divide in
modern Britain. However, the result was only one embodiment
of an increasingly fractured and polarised society. The divide
doesn't just concern voting behaviour, rather a variety of attitudes
about economics, culture and the need for belonging. These differences are often considered with a patronising smirk by a handful of people in metropolitan centres.

All too often forgotten towns, whether that be former steel
towns like Consett, once buoyant seaside resorts like Blackpool,
or mining villages that have lost their raison d'être, have problems
with welfare dependency and low-skilled, low-paid jobs. Many of
these towns have effectively become dormitories for the nearby
large cities, with limited entrepreneurialism and job creation in

the towns themselves. Residents tend to have much more of a sense of place, community and belonging than many of those who live in major cities. Their political and economic outlook is dominated by a need for economic and cultural security, rather than a desire for openness and mobility. This is a need that should be understood and acted upon by decision-makers.

These towns are suffering from a lack of good jobs, a dearth of investment, a low amount of the skills needed to prosper, poor infrastructure and a gradual 'brain drain', all of which leads to increased pressures and reduced hope. The spiral of low skill, low investment, low wage is a problem throughout the UK, but particularly in these towns, and is a result of decades of underinvestment by government and business in skills and infrastructure. As Neil O'Brien has pointed out in a report for Onward, investment in the UK has been below the OECD average in every year but one since 1960. Low skills and low investment have been a major contributor to the productivity issues that the UK economy is facing. This is particularly acute in many towns.

THE SKILLS CRISIS IN OUR TOWNS

The jobs miracle that has occurred since 2008 is important and should be acknowledged – that unemployment is at a 44-year low is a real achievement. Having a job is a crucial part of developing one's personal growth and independence, as well as a sense of dignity and pride. The substantial growth in employment and full-time work has lifted more people out of poverty and at a substantial rate. It's a formidable achievement and one that should be built on. The next challenge is to ensure that these jobs are good jobs and they bring with them the ability to upskill and to develop.

Although the so-called hourglass model of the economy – a reduction in mid-tier employment and a growth in the number of jobs at the top and bottom of the spectrum – has been a feature of most Western economies, there's substantial evidence that it has been worse in the UK. The UK economy has seen too little investment, both by government and by business, in skills, and infrastructure for many parts of the country puts them at a substantial disadvantage.

Poor investment in skills has taken its toll, and an obsession with academic qualifications has had an impact on the rest of the economy. Oxford University research by Craig Holmes found that the UK economy has shifted more towards unskilled work than most other EU countries. It found that

for every ten middle-skilled jobs that disappeared in the UK between 1996 and 2008, about 4.5 of the replacement jobs were high-skilled and 5.5 were low-skilled. In Ireland, the balance was about eight high-skilled to two low-skilled, while in France and Germany it was about seven to three. Only the Netherlands saw a similar same pattern to the UK, while Portugal did worse with no growth in high-skilled jobs at all.

Research by the Chartered Institute of Personnel and Development (CIPD) has made the level of this issue abundantly clear and has pinned the blame on both consecutive governments and business for their repeated failure to invest. It points out that for

16–24-year-olds, Britain comes close to the bottom of the OECD for literacy skills (third bottom) and numeracy skills (fourth bottom). 'It is hard to avoid the impression that many young people experience slower progression in the workplace in their first years of employment than in many other OECD economies,' says the report.

> ... the UK is distinguished in having a high share of graduates, a high share of people with low levels of qualifications, and a relatively small share of intermediate qualifications. This is in contrast to countries such as Germany, which have a much smaller share of people educated to degree level and a much larger share of intermediate skills ... The UK was ranked eleventh in 2011 by the share of those in employment who held degrees ... For those with intermediate qualifications, the UK moved in the opposite direction from twenty-fourth to twenty-eighth, roughly the same as Canada but lower than all the other major OECD economies.

According to the CIPD, UK firms invest considerably less in vocational training than their European peers. In the twenty-eight countries that make up the European Union, investment in vocational training as a percentage of labour costs is 1.6 per cent; in the UK that figure stands at 1.1 per cent, whereas it is as high as 2.5 per cent in France and 1.5 per cent in Germany. As Onward have noted, the number of people undertaking training outside the workplace has also fallen considerably in recent decades. It might be said that cultural differences between societies and economies play a part in this vocational training gap. Germany and

Switzerland, for example, have had vocational education as a key part of their culture for many years. That is not, however, a reason to suggest that our vocational system cannot be vastly improved, particularly in those parts of the country, such as those in formerly industrial areas, that built their identity and strength based on vocation and skill. Proper apprenticeships were the most important part of post-sixteen education in many areas for decades and remain part of the cultural memory of many towns. Restoring that tradition could be of great value to those towns, to young people and to the country as a whole.

THE TOWN–CITY DIVIDE

The signs of recent regeneration can be seen in many metropolitan areas. The Baltic, the Millennium Bridge and the Quayside in Newcastle, the transformed stations in Manchester and Birmingham, Millennium Square in Leeds and the virtually continental feel of the waterfront in Liverpool are all testament to regeneration money well spent. The new stations, exhibition spaces and squares stand naturally alongside the sweeping Victorian grandeur of the likes of Grey Street in Newcastle. These metropolitan centres are often accompanied by thriving higher education institutions and, at worst, reasonable links to London, even if links to other northern cities are indifferent.

Travel only a few minutes from these sparkling city centre developments, though, and you will find parts of town that are far murkier. Gateshead town centre, for example, is only a mile or so from the Baltic and the Sage in the newly christened 'Newcastle-Gateshead' – but, with its once futuristic international stadium now falling into decay, it is by no means the embodiment of glittering north-eastern regeneration. As the local newspaper puts it: 'A quick walk around the streets and you will see signs with letters missing, windows without glass and shutters pulled firmly down.' In 2016, one fifth of the stores in Gateshead town centre were empty, with the *Evening Chronicle* saying that the town had gone from 'Gateshead to Ghosthead'.

Travel a few miles further away to the likes of Ashington or Stanley and you'll find even fewer examples of successful regeneration and the 'buzz' that major metropolitan centres boast. Bookmakers abound, as do bargain stores, travel agents and, distressingly, payday loan merchants. Gateshead is connected to Newcastle and Sunderland via the Metro system, but for people in towns like Consett and Ashington there is no such option – car or, at times unreliable, local buses, which have been scaled back in recent decades, are the only option.

The government's Social Mobility Commission emphasised the importance of this divide, pointing out that many so-called cold-spots combine poor educational achievement with a weak labour market and fewer managerial and professional jobs. They argued that 'social mobility coldspots in our country are concentrated in remote rural or coastal areas and in former industrial areas … There, youngsters from disadvantaged backgrounds face far higher barriers to improved social mobility than those who grow up in cities and their surrounding hinterland.'

As Neil O'Brien has pointed out, 'within each region there is some evidence of what Alan Ehrenhalt has dubbed the "great inversion", with city centres pulling ahead of their wider regions and some of the poorest growth performance coming from peripheral towns and the outer parts of large cities'. The town–city divide was starkly illustrated, as is so often the case in modern Britain, by the result of the Brexit referendum in the north and Midlands. Whereas the large, metropolitan cities tended to lean Remain, the surrounding towns were overwhelmingly in favour of leaving the EU. In Newcastle 50.7 per cent of voters voted to stay, whereas 57 per cent of voters in Gateshead voted Leave, as did 61 per cent of voters in Sunderland and 65 per cent of voters in Middlesbrough. Remain received 60 per cent of the vote in Manchester and 50.3 per cent in Leeds. By contrast, nearby towns Wigan, Wakefield and Oldham all recorded Leave votes in excess of 60 per cent.

Polling for the Centre for Towns has highlighted the level of dislocation felt by people living in towns. Their research found that 56 per cent of people in cities feel that their area is less central to British society and only 53 per cent feel that this will be the case in the future. In contrast, some 69 per cent of voters in towns believe this, and over 71 per cent feel that this will be the case in the future. Almost 68 per cent of people in towns say that politicians 'don't care about my area' compared to 54 per cent of people in cities. Only 36 per cent of people in cities feel that their area is less well-off, compared to 53 per cent of people in towns. Towns tend to have older populations, fewer graduates, fewer people with skills, and less access to capital than cities. If something isn't done to remedy the divide, it could do even graver damage to the polity.

This divide was picked up by Labour MP Lisa Nandy, who is

also MP for Wigan, the town immortalised by Orwell and which once boasted a mighty rugby league team, which recorded a 64 per cent Leave vote. She argued that

> this consensus that began under New Labour, and was embraced by George Osborne, sees cities as engines of economic growth with surrounding towns at best anchored to them and pulled along in their prosperous wake. This is a model that has neither provided nor defended the things that matter most in our towns: thriving local high streets, shared community institutions like libraries, post offices and community pubs, good public transport, work that gives dignity and meaning, green open spaces and time with families.

Academics Will Jennings and Gerry Stoker have described this as the 'bifurcation of politics', which they regard as a global phenomenon. Christophe Guilluy has also noted a growing town–city divide in France, with his condemnation of 'bobos' (shorthand for bourgeois bohemians – a phrase also used by David Brooks) living in 'new citadels', divorced from the rest of the country.

Urgent solutions are needed to restore hope and vitality to these towns. This will come through a sustained programme of national restoration and through a radical devolution of powers to *regional and local* figures, as well as measures to incentivise investment in these areas – something we will return to in the concluding chapter.

Centre for Towns suggest that outside of the twelve 'core cities', the UK has 102 large towns (with over 75,000 residents), 243 medium-sized towns (with between 30,000 and 75,000 residents) and 559 small towns (with between 10,000 and 30,000 residents). They argue that public policy has been made primarily for twelve cities at the expense of these hundreds of towns. To return to Nandy:

> Our political system is blind to the values and experiences of people who live in our towns, wrongly treating cities as a proxy for national opinion … For far too long towns have been ignored, patronised and labelled 'left behind', allowing the assets, skills and aspirations within them to go untapped and unrealised. Those assets are alive and well in towns like Wigan, where protecting the environment and good public services are a priority, and skills, tightly knit communities and a strong sense of shared history and identity are plentiful. With the right thinking, they hold the clue to a better future.

THE NORTH–SOUTH DIVIDE

The north–south divide has been talked about so much in recent years that it has become something of a cliché. But just because something is a cliché doesn't make it any less true. Of course, parts of the north, such as central Manchester and Newcastle, have witnessed an extraordinary economic and cultural renaissance over the past decade. Equally, as sage observers such as Maurice Glasman, John Denham and Laura Sandys have pointed out, parts of the south suffer issues of deprivation that are at least as bad as in many parts of the north.

Nevertheless, they are the exceptions to the rule that prosperity and shared wealth tends to lie in the south-east of England, and the further north you go, the more likely you are to be in areas that have derived little or no benefit from this so-called shared wealth. Research by Onward has found a clear correlation between a geographically balanced economy and higher GDP per head. As they suggest, in an unbalanced economy, economic resources in some areas become overloaded, while the same resources in lagging areas are underutilised. The importance of place to people means that they don't simply move to find new opportunities, and the distances between workers and opportunities creates additional difficulties.

The starkest measure of the divide is found in governmental figures for Gross Value Added (GVA) per head, which measures the value of goods and services produced by a region. In 2016, the GVA per head in the north-east and Wales was just over £19,000. In Yorkshire it was almost £21,000. In London, the figure was well in excess of £48,000, and in the south-east was almost £29,000. The issue doesn't just lie in the gap, but the fact that it is widening; the regions with the strongest growth in recent years were those that were already ahead.

Between 2010 and 2016, the cumulative average UK growth was 12 per cent. In London, this figure stood at some 22 per cent, whereas the north-east only had a cumulative growth of 4 per cent in those six years, just behind Yorkshire, which had only 7 per cent.

These differences are also seen, depressingly, in educational and health outcomes as well. Somebody in the north is 20 per cent more likely to die early (defined as dying before the age of seventy-five) than somebody in the south. The research by the University of Manchester that uncovered this also found an alarming rise in the number of people in their twenties, thirties and forties dying in the north. In 2015, there were 49 per cent more deaths of 35–44-year-olds in the north than in the south; 29 per cent more for 25–34-year-olds. This is partially due to a worrying rise in suicides, but also a rise in cases of heart disease and other diseases linked to lifestyle and stress. In 2014, a newborn baby in Kensington and Chelsea had a life expectancy almost ten years greater than a newborn in Blackpool, with almost all of the fifty areas with lowest life expectancy being in the north-east, north-west or Wales.

There are now more than twice as many secondary schools judged to be inadequate in the north and Midlands (ninety-eight) compared with the south and east (forty-four), and of the ten worst-performing local authority areas, seven were north of The Wash. According to Sir Michael Wilshaw, the north–south divide in schooling is actually getting worse. In 2014, all the comprehensives in Yorkshire, the Humber and the north-east combined sent ninety students to Cambridge – fewer than the number (ninety-one) that came from just three schools in the south-east (Eton, Westminster and St Paul's).

The divide between the north and south, and between London and the rest, is starkly illustrated by Eurostat data about the richest and poorest regions in northern Europe. The data analysed GDP per head and took into account differing prices in different countries. It showed that 'Inner London' is the richest area in northern

Europe and the only British region in the top ten. By contrast, nine of the ten poorest regions are in the UK, with the majority being in the north. Durham and Tees Valley, South Yorkshire, Lincolnshire, Lancashire, East Yorkshire and North Lincolnshire are all among the poorest regions in northern Europe.

Successive governments have tried to tackle the north–south divide, which was clear when much of the south prospered and parts of the north struggled in the 1930s. Some of the most successful measures of industrial policy still have repercussions today. As O'Brien has argued, the development grants and capital allowances that went to Dundee shortly after the Second World War to help offset the decline of the jute industry initially helped to attract the watchmaker Timex to the town. The same factory was then used to manufacture the ZX Spectrum computer, which led to a larger than usual rate of computer ownership locally and a blossoming software programming sector. Now, many decades later, Dundee is one of the computer games design capitals of Europe, with the likes of Outplay being based there, and the course in computer games design at the local university has further encouraged the specialist cluster.

Lord Hailsham's donning of a flat cap in the 1950s was the first sign either of modern concern about the issue or of a patrician politics going out of style. The regional policies of the Macmillan and Wilson eras were well-meaning but, fundamentally, failed to bring about transformative change, especially as the latter was combined with stop-go economics and catastrophic industrial relations. Thatcher's industrial policy helped to bring the likes of Nissan to the north-east of England (where she exempted the firm from changes to capital allowances, provided favourable tax treatment for its investments and sold the land at a substantial discount) and this has been a staggering success story, with the car plant now the most productive in Europe. Enterprise zones, created in the 1980s, also had an important role to play in some areas, but they weren't combined with sufficient investment in skills or infrastructure. Despite this, the lasting impact of a flirtation with monetarism and a short-termist approach to deindustrialisation meant that the Thatcherite impact on the north can't be seen as entirely positive.

Nevertheless, some of Mrs Thatcher's ministers did see the importance of revitalising the north, with Michael Heseltine being key among them. As he recounts in his autobiography:

> I accepted that it was possible to prop up these communities in the 'worst urban areas' by increasing the flow of public money, but that didn't address the fundamental issue of concentrated poverty. We needed to attack the root cause of the problem. The teenagers with the skills, the young would-be homeowners, the strong, all those with resources to choose, had to be persuaded to stay – even to come back, live and invest – close to the areas of deprivation. It was necessary to tackle the infrastructure problems, to improve dramatically the quality of public services and to create an environment to persuade people that it was in their own interests to live and work there. In other words, one had to 'enable' these communities to compete for their place in the sun.

Heseltine's resignation over Westland, accompanied by a rise in more doctrinaire thinking about state intervention, meant that any enthusiasm for regeneration became limited. Any desire to use the power of government to boost the north probably left the government with Heseltine. Laissez-faire might have been an adequate philosophy for an already prosperous south-east, but it was singularly inadequate for the parts of the north that had suffered numerous economic blows. When Heseltine returned to government, he promised to 'intervene before breakfast, before lunch and before dinner' (and was applauded by the Conservative conference for doing so), but any such promises were quickly lost in the firefighting that engulfed John Major's government for most of its existence.

The need for northern renewal was certainly strongly felt by the Blair administration. Blair himself was a born and bred north-easterner, with a north-eastern constituency and a deeply felt love for the region. His governments were also full of fellow north-easterners, such as Alan Milburn, and senior figures with northern constituencies, such as Peter Mandelson and David Miliband.

Attempts were made to remedy the long-term unemployment of the previous decades, notably through the relocation of a number of government agencies. But these attempts failed to change the fundamental nature of northern economies, which continued to, by and large, trail behind the more prosperous south. The south-east had recovered the GDP lost during the banking crisis within two years, whereas it took parts of the north the best part of a decade.

As an *Economist* report in 2012 pointed out, private sector growth has been heavily concentrated in the south-east, whereas the state accounted for 64 per cent of the jobs created in the north between 1998 and 2007 (compared to 38 per cent in the south). They also recalled Harold Macmillan's words in 1962, when he warned that, if politicians failed to prevent 'two nations developing ... [between] a poor north and an overcrowded south ... our successors will reproach us as we reproach the Victorians for complacency about slums and ugliness'.

Although the 1997 to 2008 period had improved the major metropolitan centres of the north and helped to address some residual unemployment issues, it failed to adequately encourage the growth of a dynamic private sector in the region, didn't provide infrastructure improvements to a sufficient scale and, despite improvements, left many parts of the north vulnerable when recession hit again in 2008.

Many of these issues were acknowledged by George Osborne who, as Chancellor, championed the 'Northern Powerhouse' agenda. As he told the Tory Party conference in 2014:

I am ... the first Chancellor for almost forty years to represent a constituency in the north of England – and I can see the risk of our capital city's dominance ... It is not healthy for our country or our economy ... The answer is to build up the rest of our country. To create a Northern Powerhouse of the cities across the Pennines ... People know that the disparities between different parts of our country have grown up over many decades under governments of all colours. Let's treat people as adults and not pretend we can reverse something like this overnight. But, equally, let's not give up

and say it can't be done ... Let us choose today to make reducing
the gap between north and south, London and the rest, one of the
central ambitions of the next Conservative government.

The agenda illustrated Osborne's occasional desire to reach
beyond more conventional Thatcherite thought and see an empowering role for the state. This initiative succeeded in drawing
up unlikely alliances, including between Osborne and senior
Labour politicians in deep red cities such as Manchester and Liverpool. It has resulted in much needed directly elected mayors in
many northern cities, although the north-east, true to form, was
unable to overcome internal differences. These mayors could be
important agents of economic growth in the future, especially, as
will be considered later, if given real powers over a larger range
of economic and fiscal factors and when combined with further
devolution to surrounding towns. Providing power to towns so
that they can be part of their own economic renewal was largely
forgotten in this attempted new settlement. Although institutional progress has been made, the economic divisions remain, meaning that even more compelling political and economic action
is needed.

THE CENTURY-LONG EXODUS

London is the world's greatest city and has been a magnet for
human talent for centuries. That is something that we should be
proud of. In the few decades that London has grown and grown,
however, so other parts of the country have shrunk. The population of London increased by 15 per cent to over 8 million between

2001 and 2011. In the same period, the north-east's population only increased by around 3 per cent, and some towns also saw a net decrease in population.

While London is seen as a place that offers limitless opportunities for young people, many parts of the UK offer severely limited opportunities. Whereas London has succeeded because of its ability to network and offer professional advancement and cultural satisfaction, other parts of the UK have effectively been drained of talent. This is not London's fault – it represents a clear failure of national and local leadership to do anything to provide attractions for young people to stay and, to quote Heseltine, to come back.

The phase in which the north drove Britain's economic expansion was driven by high levels of entrepreneurship and spectacular civic leadership outside of the capital. In recent years we've seen too little of both, and national renewal requires a revival of both in the areas that need them the most. Outside of the great northern cities, the type of culturally and economically diverse and well-networked populations that promote economic success are seldom seen in some northern towns. Similarly, the north's average age has become older as younger people leave towns in search of advancement or jobs. This in itself leads to feelings of rootlessness and a diminished sense of place. Indeed, I'm one of many who had to leave my home town because the jobs simply weren't there.

A report by the Joseph Rowntree Foundation considered this population decline and what they describe as 'city decline' in greater detail. It found that ten of the twelve most struggling cities and towns were based in the north and none of the twenty-four most struggling cities and towns was based in the south (most were in the north of England; others were in the Midlands and Scotland). An Office for National Statistics (ONS) survey in 2014 showed that the population of the north of England (by which they meant the north-east, north-west and Yorkshire and the Humber) as a proportion of the overall population has reached levels last seen in the 1820s, with the north losing a quarter of its population in just over a century. In 1911, 36.5 per cent of the population were located in the north of England. By 2013, that figure had reduced to 27.9 per cent. The same report found that 56 per cent more young people were leaving the north than coming into the north. A survey by the Centre for Towns found that the population of large towns in the north-east actually fell by 7 per cent between 1981 and 2011.

Access to local capital and local talent is also in short supply. An increased centralisation of banking capital has made it more difficult for businesses in low-growth areas to get off the ground. The decline of locally rooted building societies has further hastened this. Indeed, the transformation of the Northern Counties Building Society, utterly rooted in local communities, to Northern Rock, which became an embodiment of quick buck greed, is horribly symbolic of this deterioration. The concentration of capital in the south-east of England, and particularly around London, has caused an increase of economic growth around the capital and as a result has made life much more difficult for businesses in the north. The entrepreneurial spirit that allowed northern towns and cities to drive the Industrial Revolution is often thin on the ground in many of those towns today.

THE 'GET AHEAD' AND THE 'LEFT BEHIND'

For years, one of the foundation stones of British politics has been the pursuit of 'social mobility' – something with which, along with equality of opportunity, few on the left or right could disagree with. And it was a noble pursuit – that talent rather than privilege should be rewarded. That still isn't the case, with political rhetoric on social mobility over-promising and under-delivering. The accident of birth and age-old privilege seems to be more important than merit in today's 'meritocracy'.

The second failing of this narrative is that it suggests that the only answer for an ambitious, talented young person is to somehow 'escape' their home town, dismissing those who either can't be mobile or choose not to be. For many, there is no choice other than leaving their home area to pursue jobs or careers; a more balanced economy would address that problem and also bring families and communities closer together. Social mobility is important, but it ignores other factors such as family and community that should be as important as narrow financial success. In the narrowest drive of this kind of argument, David Cameron used to talk repeatedly about winning what he called the 'global race', which meant an education system in which the best would prosper. It's also seen whenever many successful people from poorer towns talk about how they achieved their success; on too many occasions, it becomes a story of 'how I got out' or 'how I escaped', with little thought being given to how to ensure a high quality of life to those who either cannot or do not wish to do so.

In 2006, Gordon Brown predicted that the number of low-paid jobs in the UK would be as low as 600,000 by 2020, and this wasn't seen as an outrageously optimistic prediction. In truth, the number of low-paid, low-skill jobs in the UK today could be as high as 13 million.

In his excellent *Road to Somewhere*, David Goodhart has rightly emphasised that

> increasing the pay, status and productivity of people towards the bottom end of the labour market must be one of the central priorities of modern economic policy ... Policymakers ... have given far too little thought to how to promote aspiration and mobility while also valuing those who stay put, especially in the era of mass higher education. And despite the political rhetoric about opportunity for all, one nation and hard-working families, the great divergence in everyday life between good jobs – invariably graduate jobs – and basic jobs has barely been described, let alone addressed, by any of the main political parties.

If a society only celebrates success through mobility and financial success, what does that mean to those who cannot, will not or do not achieve it? Is social mobility not, then, about the talented minority jettisoning the communities in which they were born and leaving the majority behind? Surely people should be able to aspire without this meaning they have to leave their communities, and how can an emphasis on 'meritocracy' and mobility be reconciled with ensuring that all jobs have value and worth?

This is not to say that social mobility should be jettisoned as a concept. Rather, much more should be done to ensure that everybody is able to make the most of their potential. Social mobility, however, should no longer be the sole metric used; as much political energy should be invested in providing value and worth to the jobs that the majority of people will undertake.

For this to be achieved, questions must be asked about what a post-Brexit economy should look like. And one particular vision should be fought at all costs. The 'slash and burn', deregulatory approach supported by a handful of economic libertarians is one that would diminish the dignity of labour even more. In the UK, it saw its most feverish advocacy in the 2012 publication of the Beecroft Report on employment law, which would have created a hellish working life for the majority of citizens, with protection for workers shaved back to the minimal in the name of 'efficiency' and 'reducing bureaucracy' (forgetting that one man's bureaucracy is ten other men's right to paid holiday). Luckily its conclusions failed to find their way through the Lib–Con coalition's decision-making processes, but it has been rehabilitated by some as a model for what Britain could achieve outside of the EU's 'regulatory straightjacket'. At a time when millions feel that their worth at work is diminished, stripping away the rights that protect this worth could only be catastrophic and counterproductive.

Building a social contract in which not only can the best succeed, regardless of background, but in which those who do not achieve financial success have a similar stature in society, should be an aspiration for post-Brexit Britain. People should not expect to live in a country where their work and communities are constantly denigrated and devalued. Instead, they deserve to live in a society that treasures security, labour and community and which provides security and dignity through all work. Equally, politicians should aspire for a society in which an active citizenry is something pursued by the majority.

THE FETISHISATION OF UNIVERSITY AND THE HOLLOWING OUT OF TOWNS

In 2015, a year before the referendum that exposed the extent of the divide, the Department for Business, Innovation and Skills (as it was called then) carried out an analysis of the British Social Attitudes Survey, which had showed a stark, and growing, disparity between the attitudes of those who had attended university and those who had not.

The proportion of the former group has been rising considerably for decades. According to the House of Commons Library, the figure stood at 3.5 per cent in 1950, 8.4 per cent in 1970 and 19.3 per cent in 1990. Almost a third of eighteen-year-old school leavers now go on to attend university, following decades of politicians of both parties praising the university route over others.

The differing attitudes between graduates and non-graduates were many and varied.

Graduates were more likely than other educational groups to feel they had a say in what the government did and to feel it mattered which political party was in power. Graduates also have more liberal beliefs about benefits, while being far less likely to be dependent on in-work or out-of-work benefits than non-graduates. Graduates are less likely to display 'unconditional patriotism' and are more likely to support immigration (although it's argued that graduates are also less likely to be in communities or occupations that have been the most impacted by the recent wave of immigration).

All this feeds into the pastiche of 'uneducated' Leave voters that was quickly drawn up by dedicated Remainers in the months following the referendum.

That is to ignore three crucial questions. The first is whether it is healthy that the majority of voters who haven't achieved a university degree are far less likely to think that the system works in their favour. The second is whether different attitudes come from different life experiences and a form of groupthink (graduates are far more likely to mix with other graduates) or, as some imply, some form of greater wisdom that graduates achieve. And the third, probably most pertinent, question is whether the country has benefited from a system that has seen university regarded as the catch-all route for young adults.

As David Goodhart puts it, the UK university system is the only one that encourages its brightest young people to leave their home town and, in many cases, never return. Even the north's great universities don't feel the same sense of community belonging as those in continental cities, meaning that they have little desire to attract local students and little incentive to keep graduates in the town following graduation. A report for Centre for Cities showed that there is a large student outflow from towns and small cities to large cities every year, representing a transfer of economic talent from struggling towns to already vibrant cities. Leeds and Nottingham see a net inflow of over 30,000 students a year, whereas Doncaster, Wakefield and Wigan lose over 5,000 students every year. In most cases, these students never return to their home towns. The authors were right to call this a 'Great British brain drain' from towns to cities.

A report by the Higher Education Statistics Agency also found that England's regions struggle to persuade students to remain in cities after they have graduated. In the East Midlands, only 39 per cent of graduates were still in the region six months after graduating, while this number was 48 per cent in Yorkshire and 55 per cent in the north-east. By contrast, some 70 per cent of London's graduates stayed in the capital after graduating.

It's certainly true that, by international standards, UK participation in higher education was low for some time. Widening participation has, to an extent, widened opportunity. Despite increased participation from working-class young people, the bulk of the benefits have been felt by the middle class. Whereas 93 per cent of the population attend state schools, that is only the case for 64 per cent of those who attend university. And white, working-class boys in particular are under-represented in this group.

Generations of politicians were right to ensure that our population was as highly skilled as possible, particularly at a time when emerging economies outside of the West were investing heavily in their education and skills systems. However, university has since been regarded as an end in itself, with little concern for ensuring that the country has the skills it actually needs, not to mention the impact this has on towns who are losing their best young people because of an education system that encourages eighteen-year-olds to leave the areas in which they were born.

The absolute prioritisation of academic over vocational education has not delivered the skills that the country needs and has resulted in a worsening disparity of esteem between the academic and the vocational. This can only have negative consequences for the country. For years, politicians have talked about achieving parity between higher and further education, but that won't actually be achieved until those same politicians would be as happy about their own children choosing the vocational route as the academic route. For many middle-class parents, vocational education remains a good idea for other people's children. Genuine parity won't be achieved until expensive private schools are as happy to boast about their ability to help their pupils to gain entry to top vocational courses as to top universities.

A relentless expansion of higher education has meant that the UK now lags behind many major competitors in vocational education. Fewer than 20 per cent of students in the UK were enrolled in vocational education programmes in 2012. Of the European economies, only Malta and Cyprus were behind the UK in this area. In Austria, the figure was closer to 80 per cent, while it was over 50 per cent in Denmark, Norway and Finland and touching 50 per cent in Germany.

A number of reports have argued that this mismatch between vocational and academic education is having a considerable impact on the economy. A 2015 CIPD report found that over half of newly qualified graduates were working in jobs that didn't require a graduate qualification. It discovered that almost 60 per cent of graduates were in non-graduate jobs, a proportion exceeded only by Greece and Estonia. This, as the Centre for Education has found, is a trend that has been steadily worsening over time. 2013 was the first time that the number of jobs requiring a degree was greater than the number of jobs not requiring any qualifications. Some 26 per cent of jobs are now open to graduates only, up from only around one in ten in the mid-1980s. By contrast, the proportion of jobs requiring no qualifications has fallen to 23 per cent. It's clear that the labour market has not changed in a way that the expansion of higher education would have warranted.

The divides considered in this chapter intersect with each other, and an obsession with university attendance seems to have worsened the north–south divide. As David Goodhart pointed out: 'In 2014 around 45 per cent of all advertised graduate jobs in the country were London based. And despite more public debate about rebalancing Britain since the crash of 2008, the gap is getting wider.'

This is aside from the fact that huge numbers of jobs now require a degree, where in previous years they could have been careers that young people would have started straight after school. There is no equivalent of the northern European model that places an emphasis on skills from an early age. For many careers, the choice is a degree or nothing.

As we've seen, this clearly has an impact on the economy as a whole, but particularly on the struggling towns that drove the outcome of the Brexit vote. These towns need their best young people to help with recovery, and they need the right kinds of skills to move to a higher pay, higher productivity model. Through an obsession with university and academia, politicians are effectively supporting a scheme that encourages young people in struggling towns to leave in order to provide their talents to already vibrant major cities. A focus on academia has also diminished the appetite to create a vocational system that is at least on par with the academic.

THE IN-WORK POVERTY BLIGHTING OUR TOWNS

For years, the prevailing narrative about welfare was that society was somehow divided between 'grafters', infamously described by Nick Clegg as 'alarm clock Britain', and 'scroungers' who sit at home while others work. That this is a divisive straw man is indisputable. There's little evidence of widespread 'sleeping off a life on benefits' and even less that such benefits are generous enough to allow this supposed life of luxury. Clegg didn't pluck this idea from nowhere, though; it's a concept that has gradually been gaining credence over the past few decades.

A weakened social contract and a weakened sense of national cohesion has also diminished the unity that served as the basis behind the welfare state. A belief that a sizeable number of fellow citizens have not 'paid in' (the concept of paying your stamp is a redundant one) has led to a belief that the welfare system is now less firmly founded on a model of reciprocity and solidarity.

That there is some fraud in the welfare system is, of course, correct. But it's also true that the economic dislocation of the late twentieth century has produced areas where little work could be found. It's little surprise that areas of worklessness are almost co-terminus with those areas that were most reliant on heavy in-dustry and didn't see anything close to the kind of investment in retraining or new industry and infrastructure that was necessary to turn them around. Blaming the unemployed for unemploy-ment is hardly a new trait in politics – the workhouse and the Whigs' Poor Law stand as stark evidence of that – but its revival in recent years is one of the least savoury aspects of modern politics. If achieving One Nation or a revived social contract is a goal of modern politics, then it cannot start from the perspective that some of the poorest of our fellow citizens aren't a full part of that contract or are somehow gaming the system.

There are still too many people in work who struggle to make ends meet. Research by the Nuffield Foundation found that some 60 per cent of families in poverty live in a house where somebody is in work and that the risk of poverty for those in working households increased by over a quarter between 2004 and 2015.

The very communities that were once defined by secure employment and the 'job for life' are now defined by insecure, often short-term work. As James Bloodworth put it in his powerful book *Hired*, 'work for many people has gone from being a source of pride to a relentless and dehumanising assault on their dignity'.

In *Hired*, Bloodworth recounted his experience of working in a distribution factory, where the balance between employer and worker had become hugely disjointed:

> The place had the atmosphere of what I imagined a prison would feel like. Most of the rules were concerned with petty theft. You had to pass in and out of gigantic airport-style security gates at the end of every shift and each time you went on a break or needed to use the toilet. It could take ten or fifteen minutes to pass through these huge metal scanners. You were never paid for the time you spent waiting to have your pockets checked.

Each worker in this distribution centre is given a small electronic device, which monitors their movement and activity, with frequent warnings to improve work rate and productivity. It's hard to read accounts like Bloodworth's and others' and not conclude that, in many workplaces, workers have lost their sense of agency and control. While the 'take back control' slogan used by the Leave campaign was focused on the EU, it clearly exhibited an understanding of the lack of 'control' felt by many workers in other parts of their life.

A combination of stagnating wages, minimal skills investment, the loss of industry in what were once 'mono-industrial' towns and the decline of trade unions has helped to increase the level of insecurity felt by many. At the same time, the value and worth attached to many occupations has decreased. In towns like Consett, a skilled welder was seen as a valued and important job. The replacement of these occupations with call-centre or box-packing work is not a like-for-like replacement. Too many of those towns lack both the infrastructure and the entrepreneurialism that will create more highly valued jobs for communities.

The changing nature of work and other pressures, notably rent expenses, have damaged the 'hard work is rewarded' narrative beloved of so many. Few work as hard as many in the low-paid echelons of society, who often have to juggle a number of stressful and demeaning jobs, which in turn diminishes the amount of time they have to spend in their family and community lives.

Much of the work at the lower end of the spectrum isn't just poorly paid, it's also desperately insecure and attached to poor working conditions. The worst example of so-called zero-hours contracts sees some workers not knowing until the morning whether they will be needed for work that day.

My grandads and their peers, working in the mines and

steelworks of the Consett area, had to work hard jobs (so hard that, as I've previously mentioned, a life down the mine meant that they both had a tragically early death caused by work-related illness). They were part, however, of a strong community. They benefited from annual holiday, strong representation, gradually shorter working hours and increasingly better conditions at work. This was undoubtedly progress, and it's hard not to feel that this progress has been eroded for many over the past few years. A rise of insecure agency work has removed dignity and security for some in the labour market, also making it more difficult to maintain the link between working hard and getting by. As discussed earlier, this insecure, low-skilled work issue is directly linked to low public and private sector investment in skills.

Strong trade unions were a central part of the working world inhabited by my grandparents. They play no part at all in the landscape of many low-paid workers today. This failure should be placed squarely at the door of the trade union movement itself. The surge of activism and militancy in the 1960s and '70s saw the social contract weakened and meant that unions were actually further away from fulfilling their defining role, with a growing view that these unions were 'out of control'.

Since their membership peak in the 1970s, trade unions have retreated squarely into a public sector comfort zone. To many younger workers and workers in insecure jobs in the private sector, trade unions have no relevance to their lives at all, and it is these workers who would benefit the most from effective unions. Trade unions have failed to make themselves seem relevant to many in the private sector and have often squandered opportunities to increase this relevance. Rather than talk about practical relevance, some trade union leaders are too easily engaged in left-wing hobby horses or unrelated foreign policy issues (Venezuela, Cuba and Israel tend to top the list) that deter potential members.

THE HOUSING CRISIS GRIPPING OUR TOWNS

The divide between homeowners and renters is one of the biggest drivers of inequality and reaffirms the divide between age and class that is becoming such a dominant feature of British society. While homeownership looked like it might become the norm a few decades ago, among younger people and those on low incomes it is now becoming an exception. Despite the cliché that this is just a 'London' or a south-eastern issue, towns throughout the country have seen a fall in homeownership and, notably, a rise in private renting, as is shown in the table below. This has been accompanied by more people paying substantial sums to live in poor-quality, insecure private rented housing.

Town	Fall in home ownership 2001–2018	Rise in private renting 2001–2018
Barnsley	3 per cent	8 per cent
Blackpool	26 per cent	18 per cent
Consett	13 per cent	16 per cent
Doncaster	16 per cent	23 per cent
Gateshead	6 per cent	12 per cent
Harlow	24 per cent	22 per cent
Sunderland	9 per cent	18 per cent
Wakefield	5 per cent	8 per cent
Wigan	11 per cent	15 per cent
England average	*14 per cent*	*17 per cent*

Homeownership is something that should be valued, defended and spread as widely as possible. In many ways, by the beginning of this century, that argument seemed to have been won. It now needs to be refought. For one, homeownership provides a sense of belonging to a community. It also provides a feeling that people have a stake in both the economy and society. This was a case made early in the twentieth century by Noel Skelton, part of a generation of reforming Tories nicknamed the YMCA (Harold Macmillan was another), who made the case for a popular Toryism that involved homeownership. His case seems as important today as it was then:

> ... to give the wage earner property and status; to bridge the economic gulf set between Labour and Capital; to present a view of life in which private property ... will be recognised as the essential vehicle for the moral and economic progress of the individual; these are the tasks which the opportunity, the problem, and its own principles alike call Conservatism to perform in the new era.

Homeownership in the UK is at almost 65 per cent, which is below the EU average and well below the levels of 84 per cent in Norway, 67 per cent in Holland and 69 per cent in Sweden. At the same time, the level of private renting has increased enormously, almost doubling in the past decade. There are now 11 million private renters, including 1.5 million families with children stuck privately renting.

This stark decline of homeownership has taken place among those on low incomes. More of that group now rent privately than own their own home and the proportion of first-time buyers on low incomes halved between 2003 and 2015, from 14.1 per cent to 7.1 per cent. The number of first-time buyers on the lowest income is now only 1.7 per cent. Homeownership is increasingly becoming the preserve of wealthier people – 42 per cent of first-time buyers are those on the highest incomes, compared to 34 per cent in 2003–04.

This is a problem affecting the middle, but it is most profoundly hitting those on lower incomes. The divide in homeownership is now a significant driver of inequality, with the issue of a low-wage economy, which is particularly notable in our towns, being compounded by the fact that a greater proportion of these wages is being hoovered up by rent. This also creates the perverse situation where the state is subsidising poor-quality private rented accommodation through the housing benefit (the annual housing benefit bill is as high as £29 billion), while the goal of a property-owning democracy seems further away than ever.

Many of the same families in our towns end up being 'stuck' in low-quality, high-cost private rented accommodation and are, instead, unable to find a way onto the housing ladder. For many, such a goal seems a mirage. Fifty-two per cent of private renters on the national living wage and below want to own but don't think they ever will. Forty-four per cent of private renters earning £15,000 to £24,000 feel the same way.

There are many reasons behind the above decline in home-ownership, but two key factors are what could be called a 'double whammy': high house prices and high rents. House prices have massively outstripped wages over recent decades. Shelter research showed that 'if wages had risen as fast as house prices had, an average couple with children would earn an extra £44,000 a year. An average single person in England would have an extra £29,000 on top of their salary while an average couple without children would have an extra £59,000.'

As important is the second factor: high private rents. In each region of the country, rents have increased by more than inflation. After tax, private renters in England pay 47 per cent of their income in rent. Tax cuts alone would not sufficiently alter this: even before tax, 38 per cent of private renters' salary goes on rent outside London. Moreover, these are average figures: affordability is likely to be even worse at the lower end of the income spectrum.

These increased levels of private rent expenditure leave many aspiring homeowners on low incomes unable to save anything up towards a deposit on a home of their own at the end of the month. As YouGov/Shelter research has found, roughly half of such private renters report this to be the case – and, again, it's likely to be even more acute for those on low incomes.

Many English towns haven't just been affected by a crisis of supply and affordability; they've also been impacted by a crisis of design. Low- or high-rise tower blocks have tended to replace houses with gardens and the natural communal areas offered by streets. This shift was an international tragedy, which we have only recently started to come to terms with.

Addressing all of these issues – the decline of homeownership, the growth of private renting and the poor design of much new housing – is essential to so many of our forgotten towns.

CUT OFF? THE POOR TRANSPORT LINKS
HOBBLING OUR FORGOTTEN TOWNS

The World Economic Forum produces annual surveys of the global infrastructure picture and this confirms the need for prioritisation of infrastructure spending. Its most recent survey showed that the UK's overall infrastructure is twenty-seventh in the world, with roads being twenty-seventh and railways nineteenth. Globally, the most successful urban centres are the ones that are highly 'networked' within regions and sub-regions, with great transport connectivity and facilities such as high-speed broadband.

Analysis of how infrastructure cash has been spent in recent years underlines how spending decisions have made regional inequalities worse. Research by IPPR North has shown that regional inequalities in transport spending are long-lasting and are likely to continue over the coming years. They found that from 2017/18, some £4,155 per capita is due to be spent on transport infrastructure in London, compared to just £1,600 in the north as a whole. Planned spend per person in London is almost five times that in Yorkshire (£844 per capita) or the north-east (£855 per capita).

Contrast the fortunes of somebody living in Consett in 2019 with somebody living in London at the same time. In Consett, local roads have been suffering for years, with potholes growing increasingly worse due to a sequence of severe winters. A public transport journey from Consett to Manchester covers only 116 miles but could take an astonishing three hours and forty-five minutes. This would include a 56-minute bus journey and a train that takes almost two hours.

Bus services have also been cut back across the north. This might

seem a parochial issue to people who rely on London's vast Tube
network, but it's less so in those towns, such as Consett, that have
no railway station and for which buses are the only form of public
transport. What's more, a BBC report has found that the bus network in the UK has declined by some 8 per cent within a decade.

Research for the Campaign for Better Transport showed that
in the six years leading up to 2017, spending on buses in County
Durham was cut by 30 per cent. In other northern towns this was
much higher. For example, in Hartlepool and Middlesbrough, the
budget for buses was cut completely, and in Blackburn it was cut
by 68 per cent. These buses are also hugely expensive, particularly
given the proliferation of low-paid work. For example, a bus fare
between Consett and Durham is an astonishing £5.30, whereas a
single bus journey in London would cost £1.50.

In contrast, a London resident has seen dramatic investment in
their transport infrastructure in recent years. Crossrail will allow
rapid journeys across the south-east, including to Heathrow Airport. The first benefits of HS2 will be felt in the capital, which
has also benefited from investment in ThamesLink and expansion
to the Jubilee and Northern lines. The impact of HS2 could also
strengthen the centrifugal pull of London, rather than enhancing
the links between towns and cities in the north.

This is not to argue that London, the world's greatest city,
shouldn't have seen transport investment. Rather, it is to argue
that the overall weight of such investment in recent years has been
to widen divides and entrench inequalities. That approach must
change. With his announcement of Crossrail for the north, Boris
Johnson seems to have indicated that the approach is changing.

DIMINISHED HIGH STREETS
AND COMMUNITY SPACES

The decline of the high street has been an obsession of policy makers for decades and is symbolic of a bigger problem – the decline of communal institutions that once brought people together. The modern high street in many towns is all too often a collection of charity shops, bargain or pound stores, bookmakers, travel agents and pawn shops. Shops selling cut-price vitamins and toiletries are also ubiquitous. In many towns, national chains of one kind or another dominate, and local shopkeepers have long ago closed their shutters.

Declining high streets is only one part of the story, though. Communal institutions have been dwindling, too, giving people fewer reasons to visit the town centre. While metropolitan cities are increasingly making imaginative use of communal spaces and green spaces, many town centres are rapidly diminishing.

A quarter of pubs have closed since the turn of the century and with them their role as community hubs. This is also the case with the decline of community institutions such as working men's clubs, which have seen their number reduced from 5,000 in the 1970s to little more than 1,000 today. A marked decline in institutions such as youth clubs and community centres can be added to this list – all places that existed to bring people together and encouraged us to mix with people from different walks of life. Libraries have also been the victims of cuts and a declining sense of community.

Organised religion, another institution that once served to bond communities, has been in decline for decades. This is particularly the case with the Methodist Church, which used to have such a hold on working-class towns, to the extent that Harold Wilson said that the Labour Party owed 'more to Methodism than to Marx' and E. P. Thompson could argue that the reason for the UK not following other European countries in an eighteenth- or nineteenth-century revolution was the influence of Methodism on working-class towns. There were almost 850,000 members of Methodist branches in the early twentieth century; this was still over half a million in the 1970s and over 400,000 in the 1980s, but by 2016 that number had fallen to little more than 185,000.

Academics call this building of strong community links 'social capital', and its decline – whether caused by a reduction in shops, pubs, Post Offices or community centres – really does matter. The decline in social capital can be seen in every boarded-up shop, every closed pub and every Methodist chapel that's been convert-ed into a private home. In each of these instances, society has become a little more atomised and a little less cohesive.

As John Harris, one of the few modern journalists who gen-uinely understands the issues facing many communities, argues:

There is also a clear sense of something every bit as fundamental: the decline of shared spaces, and the way we seem to be splintering into ever-smaller social niches. Many local businesses and institu-tions that depend on attracting a wide range of people are fading away … In the Britain of 2018, one question for the kind of people who have probably never set foot in their local boozer has become a cliché: do you know anyone who voted leave? Soon enough, it may be superseded by an even more alarming one: do you know anyone who isn't exactly like you?

THE NEW CLASS DIVIDES SHUTTING
OUT OUR FORGOTTEN TOWNS

Britain is one of the most class-obsessed countries under the sun. That was what George Orwell wrote in 'The Lion and the Unicorn', and it's tempting to argue that little has positively changed since it was published in 1941. Outright snobbery is no longer acceptable, of course, although, as Owen Jones perceptively pointed out, the word 'chav' has become symbolic of a demonisation of parts of working-class life.

In fact, it can also be said that society might actually be more divided and more stratified than at any time since the Second World War. The devastating impact of war and depression shaped the country for decades – the upper class as much as the working class. Harold Macmillan is just one example of a generation of 'patricians' whose views were altered by his experiences during these years. He served in the trenches with working-class men and also served as the MP for Stockton – a town that was hit particularly hard by the post-1929 downturn. His example was not unique. Despite the Blackadder-style myth of the posh letting the poor be slaughtered, the truth was that the sacrifice of the upper classes was as remarkable as that of the rest of the country.

A shared sense of danger and experience, including of National Service, during peacetime meant that rich and poor weren't totally alien to each other. Snobbery and social differences were rife, but there were more shared memories and commonality then than now.

Today there is the chance that people who attend the top private schools will have no reason to interact with the poorest, or those in the insecure jobs discussed earlier. Many of the wealthiest people will never have been to the towns we discuss here. Nor are they likely to socialise with many people who are from those towns.

A controversial app launched in 2017 allowed people who had been to private schools to date other people who had been to private schools. The app, called 'Toffee', was founded on the basis that 'people who hold similar views and values, and have shared the same life experiences (such as going through the same education system), are more likely to be attracted to each other and stick together.' Even if the app was a slightly delayed April Fool (that still isn't clear), its raison d'être clearly sums up the divide between privately educated and the rest and why that matters. It might seem a trivial example, but it stands as an example of a desire for social demarcation and the reality of two nations.

Before his resignation in late 2017, Alan Milburn had done the nation a great service in chronicling this demarcation on an annual basis during his chairmanship of the government's Social Mobility Commission. Each year the Commission published its 'State of the Nation' report on social mobility, which continued to make depressing reading with its repeated descriptions of why, in Milburn's words, 'birth not worth' is a defining factor in whether people succeed in modern Britain.

Milburn started his final report with the words, 'Britain is a deeply divided nation.' Looking at the evidence contained in the report, it's difficult to disagree with these words:

> The growing sense that we have become an us and them society is deeply corrosive of our cohesion as a nation. The analysis in this

report substantiates the sense of political alienation and social re-
sentment that so many parts of modern Britain feel. Whole tracts
of our country feel left behind, because they are. Whole communities feel that the benefits of globalisation have passed them
by, because they have. Whole sections of society feel they are not
getting a fair chance to succeed, because they are not. It cannot go
on like this. If we want a genuinely United Kingdom, not an ever
more divided one, a new approach will be needed.

Reports over recent years have also found that stark social class
differences are clear from a very early age. In the past decade,
500,000 poorer children were not 'school-ready'* by the age of
five. Over the past five years, 1.2 million sixteen-year-olds, disproportionately from low-income backgrounds, have left school
without five good GCSEs. Just 5 per cent of children eligible
for free school meals achieved five A grades at GCSE. Class is a
more reliable indicator of educational achievement than gender
or ethnicity.

The pattern seems clear. The divide between the poorest and
the rest of society is entrenched by the age of five. By the age
of sixteen, children from poorer backgrounds have fallen behind
their wealthier compatriots. And by the age of eighteen, those
who have attended fee-paying schools have leapt ahead of everybody else and this gap is maintained for the rest of their lives.
The twin issues of poverty on the one hand and privilege on the

---

* The Department for Education define 'school-ready' as having sufficient ability in
communication and language; physical development; personal, social and emotional
development; literacy and maths.

other combine to maintain a society that starts out unfair and only becomes more so.

This is not a new issue of course. In the early 1960s, that great lost hope of the Tory One Nation tradition, Iain Macleod, gave a tremendous speech in which he warned of the stratification of society. He argued that a just society is one 'which can confidently invite the men and women who compose it to make their own way in the world, because no reasonable opportunity is denied them. You cannot ask men and women to stand on their own two feet if you give them no ground to stand on.'

At its crudest, British society continues to be one that is tilted in favour of the wealthy and against the poorest – unintelligent rich kids are much more likely to succeed than bright poor kids. As we've said, this is not a new issue, but that shouldn't make tackling it any less urgent. If it isn't addressed, British society will be operating at far less than its full potential. Some argue that taking action to tackle the iniquity would be going against the principle of 'meritocracy'. However, this would require belief in the absurd myth that the 7 per cent of the population lucky enough to have parents able to afford private education are also, by coincidence, the brightest and the best. That is self-evident folly.

Ensuring that professions are not a closed shop should, of course, be done in unison with raising the prestige of blue-collar work. But that shouldn't mean that more can't be done to open up top professional jobs as well.

Successive governments have taken steps to improve education in poorer areas and real progress has been made. My own school was transformed from a failing school, with the worst academic record in County Durham, to one of the best under Tony Blair's academy programme. The so-called London Challenge led to dramatic improvements in state schools in the capital. But it's resoundingly clear that more needs to be done – being born poor remains far too great a predictor of growing up poor and dying poor, and this is more the case than in almost every other European country.

HEALING THE DIVIDE?

Britain is a divided nation. The Brexit referendum didn't cause the divide, but it did serve to expose it. Many parts of the country feel that the economy has stopped working in their interests and, in many ways, it has. Equally, politics has tended to entrench these divides rather than heal them, with old political ideology continuing to be espoused by many, despite the public mood and changing public realities. People don't want to hear more of the dogma that they thought they rejected in 2016. Instead, they want to hear about how politicians understand their concerns and how their politics will improve their day-to-day lives.

The town–city divide encapsulates this sense of two nations. There is probably as little social or economic understanding between Bayswater and places like Consett now than there has been for many decades. To again quote Disraeli, to many in post-Brexit Britain, it does feel like we are 'dwellers in different zones or inhabitants of different planets'. Renewed politics needs to prioritise creating a renewed One Nation.

CHAPTER THREE

ENGLAND'S FORGOTTEN VOTERS

The heirs of Nelson and of Cromwell are not in the House of Lords.
They are in the fields and the streets, in the factories and the armed
forces, in the four-ale bar and the suburban back garden; and at
present they are still kept under by a generation of ghosts.
— GEORGE ORWELL, 'THE LION AND THE UNICORN'

When you ain't got nothing, you've got nothing to lose.
— BOB DYLAN, 'LIKE A ROLLING STONE'

Redhills in Durham is one of the most beautiful buildings in one of England's most stunning cities. It's otherwise known as the Miners' Hall and is still home to the Durham Miners' Association. Its grandeur is testament to the once mighty nature of the Durham coalfield.

Inside the Miners' Hall sits the so-called Pitmens' Parliament – the chamber in which the union would meet to discuss important issues of the day. There are 297 seats in this debating chamber, representing the 297 pits in operation in the Durham coalfield when the chamber was first built. Each pit would send one representative to meetings of the Pitmens' Parliament and decisions made here would have substantial repercussions on national politics.

Herbert Morrison's 'the Durham miners won't wear it' wasn't just a throwaway remark; it was an expression of the real power held by workers in the north-east of England. In the decades that have gone by, the grandchildren and great-grandchildren of those Durham miners have found their views ignored and their concerns have gone from central to peripheral.

This goes alongside the crisis discussed in the previous chapter, that England's towns are facing an increase of low-skill, low-pay jobs, poor infrastructure, a decline in entrepreneurialism and an exodus of many talented young people. Wealth and opportunity in the UK have tended to concentrate in major cities, while towns and coastal areas have tended to be cut off.

Many people who live in these cut-off areas feel that their views aren't sufficiently heard in the corridors of power and their opinions are often excluded from political parties dominated by an economic and identity liberalism that is largely metropolitan and defensive of the status quo. The Brexit result clearly showed, however, that there is a clear disconnect between how politicians think, behave and act compared to a great bulk of the general population.

Voters in England's forgotten towns have become more and more disengaged from the political process. In some of these towns, turnout in general elections has barely been above 50 per cent as voters become increasingly likely to think that the political process doesn't reflect or benefit them. In a 2012 survey, some 82 per cent of people agreed with the statement 'politicians don't understand the real world at all'. A poll in 2019 found that over 80 per cent of voters thought that politicians don't listen to ordinary people.

Disengagement among working-class voters is clearly seen in turnout and political involvement. This had seen a marked divergence in voting behaviour and the growth of a so-called turnout 'class gap'. This disengagement has meant that many working-class people have stopped voting altogether, with the 'gap' in voting becoming a chasm. In 1992, the voting gap between the proportion of professionals who voted and the skilled working class who voted was 8 per cent. By 2010, this gap had increased to 18 per cent and remained at that level in 2015.

Many of these disengaged voters were energised by the Brexit referendum. Ipsos estimated that 64 per cent of unskilled workers voted in the 2016 referendum, compared to 57 per cent in the election a year earlier. There was a similar turnout rise among skilled working-class voters.

The referendum included full-throated support for the European Union from almost the entire business and financial establishment and a succession of foreign leaders and dignitaries – all of which were confident that the case for EU membership was both abundant and self-evident. According to a Political Studies Association survey, 97 per cent of journalists, 92 per cent of pollsters and 87 per cent of academics thought that Britain would vote to stay in the EU. Communities were told about the prosperity that EU membership had achieved for the country in recent decades and were warned not to jeopardise it. This wasn't the way that these communities had seen the past few decades at all. Many had seen a gradual reduction in economic vibrancy and lasting economic and social problems that hadn't been adequately tackled. Three million people who hadn't voted in the 2015 general election came out to vote a year later – from this we can only surmise that the referendum gave them what they believed was an opportunity to change things in a way that general elections hadn't done for generations.

In an article published shortly before the referendum, Dr Lisa McKenzie argued that the vote had opened up a 'Pandora's box of working-class anger and frustration', which had 'unnerved' much of the political class. As she pointed out, these working-class voices had seldom been heard outside of their own communities, and many voters had stopped voting in general elections, believing that change was unlikely. During the campaign, voters in marginalised areas

> stopped listening to politicians and to Westminster, and they are doing what every politician fears: they are using their own experiences in judging what is working for and against them ... Working-class people in the UK can see a possibility that something might change for them if they vote to leave the EU.

Commenting on the article in his excellent *Long Road from Jarrow*, Stuart Maconie said:

> In the midst of the post-Brexit hand wringing, navel-gazing and fist shaking, this struck a bracing chord. Whilst no Brexiteer, I'd been dismayed at how whole areas of Britain and all kinds of people I'd grown up with and lived with could be so easily, so lazily, so insultingly, dismissed.

Newcastle was the only local authority area in the north-east to vote Remain, and only by 1 per cent. In other north-eastern local authorities, Sunderland voted to leave by 23 per cent, Gateshead and Durham by 15 per cent, Northumberland by 8 per cent and Middlesbrough by over 30 per cent. In all cases, turnout was considerably higher than in any general election of recent times. The contrast between the English turnout of 73 per cent in the referendum and the 66 per cent in the election a year earlier was repeated across the north.

For some time, politicians have failed to offer a coherent or compelling vision for these towns. And in the cases where they have provided vision, they have generally failed to fulfil it. Local Labour MPs have largely depended on 'not being Tories', relying on anti-Tory sentiment or memories of the 1980s as adequate reasons to vote for them.

Anti-Tory rhetoric is no substitute for local or regional ambition and counts for less over time as no improvement in day-to-day conditions is felt. It should be little surprise that the first political event where anti-Tory rhetoric wasn't relevant was the first political event for many decades in which thousands of working-class voters took an active part. Many communities had grown weary of being taken for granted and tired of a political machine that depended on them to always vote 'in the right way'. Brexit represented a rare occasion in which working-class voters, particularly in towns, thought that they could make a difference in a politics that seldom reflected their concerns.

As academics Matthew Goodwin and Roger Eatwell have made clear, the Brexit vote did not have a single, simplistic explanation.

Nevertheless, it clearly, at least in part, represented a cry of anger from people who felt that the existing system wasn't working for them. As the National Centre for Social Research found in its analysis of the result, 70 per cent of people finding it 'difficult to manage successfully' and 60 per cent of those 'just getting by' ended up voting Leave, as did 73 per cent of those who felt that 'Britain has got a lot worse in the past ten years.' Seventy-six per cent of those who said that things had 'got a lot worse for me compared to other people' voted for Brexit.

It would be a mistake, however, to see the EU as the sole, or even the primary, factor behind people's discontent in 'left-behind' towns. The key element was a perception of lost power, agency and control. Politicians shouldn't see EU withdrawal as a panacea. Rather, they should view the referendum result as a warning that people in forgotten towns expect their voices and concerns to be both represented and listened to and for real change to occur.

ELITE GROUPTHINK AND THE LIBERAL ANXIETY

The response to the referendum result was almost as remarkable as the result itself, with Remain campaigners looking to reassure themselves that it was down to a mixture of Russian meddling, lying politicians and uneducated voters. It was the first time for decades that middle-class liberal voters had seen their worldview questioned, leading to a crisis of confidence and a belief that the result could only be explained by ulterior motives or an inability of 'Leave' voters to fully comprehend the 'facts'. In some cases, the language of the debates around the Reform Acts made an unwelcome and unexpected return to politics, with one commentator calling for a franchise restriction and social media being awash with people complaining about the votes of the 'thick'.

Other commentators have pointed to the rise of 'Brexit Anxiety Disorder', with the liberal middle classes now feeling the same lack of 'control' that had been felt for decades by working-class voters. In essence, wealthier, professional and educated voters, who generally live in cities, effectively feel that the Brexit result and the subsequent direction of the country were things over which they had little control. This was a rude awakening for a social group who had effectively driven the direction of the country for decades.

This follows on from a belief among generally middle-class metropolitan liberals that they are uniquely well-informed and able to judge issues more effectively than those who voted Leave in the referendum. It is reflected by a groupthink about a variety of issues – including electoral reform, free movement of labour, and EU federalism – that tends to be well represented in the media and in politics but unreflective of broader societal views. As James Kanagasooriam has shown, and as is reflected in the few areas (Oxford, Cambridge, Edinburgh) that voted in favour of the Alternative Vote in 2011, such views tend to be geographically concentrated in a handful of university cities.

Such a groupthink has also resulted in a number of instances where popular opinion has proved considerably shrewder than apparently better-informed elite opinion. This includes issues that have had a profound impact on modern Britain. Other than for a brief blip, the majority of voters always opposed British participation in the Iraq War, whereas MPs endorsed the invasion. There was cross-party support for the catastrophe of the Exchange Rate Mechanism (ERM) membership, which was also backed by trade unions, business organisations and media commentators, but this support was never reflected among the general public.

Senior figures in all parties supported membership of the single currency, but no poll showed majority support for this within the British public. Similarly, there has always been public support for the building of more council housing, even though elite opinion for some time regarded council housing as belonging in the past. The public was never as infatuated with the power of finance or the City of London as leading MPs have been. Elite opinion shouldn't be restricted to leading MPs. The Confederation of British Industry, for example, was strongly in support of both ERM membership and membership of the euro.

Regarding some of the most important decisions the country has faced in recent decades, elite opinion has been subject to an all-pervading groupthink, which is too little punctured by the worldview of England's towns. In so many of these cases, the often-derided voice of public opinion has usually been considerably wiser than the 'learned' voices of elite opinion.

THE DECLINE OF WORKING-CLASS MPS

Such groupthink is created by the narrowness of the social and ideological backgrounds of members of the political class. Recent decades have seen a decline in the number of MPs from non-academic and from non-white-collar backgrounds. This has an inevitable impact on the priorities of those engaged in politics.

The decline of working-class MPs is put into context when you consider that every Prime Minister from Harold Wilson to John Major was educated in a state school. Post-war Cabinets have also been dominated by people from working-class backgrounds, from Ernest Bevin and Nye Bevan to Norman Tebbit and Alan Johnson.

In recent years, people from wealthier backgrounds have tended to play a more dominant role in politics. Both Tony Blair and David Cameron came from highly privileged backgrounds, as did most of the latter's coterie – with 62 per cent of the coalition Cabinet and 50 per cent of the 2015 Cabinet coming from private schools. The 2018 Cabinet saw this number reduced to 34 per cent, but private schools were still represented five times more in the Cabinet than in the population at large. Figures from the House of Commons Library show that 20 per cent of all MPs and some 44 per cent of Conservative MPs were educated at private schools.

A similar level of detachment from society as a whole can be seen when looking at how many MPs attended university. Whereas only a third of eighteen-year-olds attend university, some 84 per cent of MPs are university educated. This includes 84 per cent of Labour MPs, compared to only two thirds when Tony Blair was first elected.

Some might retort that it is important that we have MPs who have a good education. That ignores the fact that many of our most successful politicians, such as Disraeli, Lloyd George, Ernest Bevin and Nye Bevan, did not attend university. Of course, graduates should be represented in the Commons, but should they really be three times more represented there than they are in the population as a whole?

The change in the makeup of Parliament can be shown more

dramatically when we consider the occupations of MPs before being elected to Parliament. In 1979, almost 16 per cent of MPs came from manual work backgrounds. This figure remained as high as 9 per cent in 1997 but has now fallen to a mere 3 per cent. By contrast, the proportion of people who had worked for political parties has exploded from 3 per cent to over 7 per cent. Quite simply, this suggests that MPs are coming from a narrower pool, with a narrower set of views and narrower life experiences.

Parliament has made great strides in improving representation of various groups who have historically been badly unrepresented. For example, the 2017 Parliament contained the highest ever number of female MPs, as well as non-white and LGBT members. That is undoubtedly a positive development. However, in the same time period, Parliament seems to have gone backwards in terms of making sure that people from left-behind towns and manual professions are represented.

Concurrent with this 'echo chamber' impact of modern politics has been the rise of a specific political class. This came to a head in the 2015 election, when all three party leaders were incredibly young by historical standards and none of them had really held a job outside of politics (other than David Cameron's brief time working in communications). All had followed the well-travelled route from Oxbridge to becoming special advisers, MPs at a young age, and then Cabinet ministers. Real-world experience was limited and experience of the towns miles away from Oxbridge or Westminster was slim. Former Labour Cabinet minister Hazel Blears has talked about how she wrote an article criticising this familiar career path for senior politicians. The following morning, she was taken aside by several Cabinet colleagues who were fearful that the article was aimed specifically at them.

It also raises the issue of a one-dimensional approach to diversity. For example, does a woman from Consett feel better represented by a male factory worker from the same town or by a woman from an expensive private school who had previously worked as an investment banker? Would a poor black boy growing up in Brixton feel adequately represented by a black MP with a privileged education and wealthy background? Such questions show that a one-dimensional approach to parliamentary diversity is deeply unsatisfactory. That is before considering the point that many on the left regard white-collar jobs in the trade union movement as somehow equivalent to a working-class background.

Being a political candidate is also an expensive business. Candidates are expected to devote a huge amount of time and money to their role. Put together, the costs of travel, accommodation and, in many cases, lost earnings can be enormous. As Isabel Hardman recently set out in *Why We Get the Wrong Politicians*, this means that politics is becoming a profession for the independently wealthy or the trade-union-funded, shutting out people from other backgrounds and creating a narrower political cadre.

The influence of donor power also means that there are often many more influential voices in politics than those from working-class towns. Donors are regarded with a reverence that is deeply unhealthy for the body politic. Newspaper stories are often accompanied with talks of 'donor concerns' about the actions of politicians and the implicit threat that their largesse will be removed if political policies aren't changed.

Corporate interests are also not shy about wielding their power. Theresa May, upon becoming Prime Minister, made having workers on boards one of the centrepieces of her initial offering, both in her leadership campaign and in her initial address to the nation from the steps of Downing Street. The policy was extremely popular with the public but was quickly dropped due to the opposition of corporate donors.

Critics are also right to point out that wealthy businessmen and women aren't the only donors with cards on the table. Trade unions now represent by far the biggest donors to the Labour Party. Indeed, the frantic nature of the activities of Lord Levy was probably connected to a desire to break this link. Some would point out that Labour was formed by the unions and they collectively represent several million members. This is a valid point, but it's difficult to see how the continued outsize influence of either union leaders (elected with a derisory turnout and tending to be unrepresentative of member views) or the super wealthy can be healthy for democracy at large.

Looking around the world of party fundraising events, it's hard not to consider what this would mean to voters in places like Consett, who feel that political parties have shut them out. Unless these towns are located in marginal constituencies (and most of them are not), they're unlikely to receive regular visits from senior politicians. The way in which fundraising is conducted and money is raised in British politics amplifies a disconnect that already exists. It provides a perverse incentive for politicians to listen to the views of the already rich and powerful and makes it less likely that they will have time to hear the views of the majority.

It creates a sense that politics is a closed shop and tends to narrow the avenues in which politics happens and policy is made.

Few at thousand-pound-a-ticket balls are likely to have first-hand experience at the iniquities of low pay, insecure work or being treated badly at the hands of a rogue landlord. By contrast, cuts in taxes for the wealthy are likely to find high levels of support. This further shuts out the most important voices and amplifies some of the most vocal, purely on account of their wealth. It creates a politics that gives greater priority to Bayswater and Chelsea over Consett and Doncaster.

When people see politicians that don't seem to share their accents, their life experiences, their background or their views, they are more likely to become disengaged from and disenchanted with politics and feel that it is not adequately representing them.

UNREPRESENTED OPINIONS AND THE PARADOX OF THE CENTRE GROUND

Many MPs who represent working-class parts of the country tend to have little sympathy for many of the values of their constituents. Labour MPs, for example, may agree with their constituents on the need for greater state intervention in the economy, but might differ when it comes to issues such as immigration, welfare, multiculturalism and EU membership.

Equally, as many have pointed out, there is a stark shortage, particularly on the Conservative side of the House, but also on the Labour benches, of those MPs with an understanding of poverty or deprivation. Few have experience of life in social housing or waiting on the social housing waiting list, and few have experience of relying on tax credits or housing benefits to subsidise their income enough to be able to support their family. This level of understanding is bound to have an impact on policy-making.

This doesn't just create a situation where the social situation of many people in England's towns is unrepresented in politics, but also where widely held political worldviews are under-represented. In short, the worldview of the metropolitan middle class – generally economically and socially liberal – is more than adequately represented on the green benches. (Since the rise of Corbynism, there has also been a growth in the ranks of old-style socialists.)

What is missing, however, is the political bloc that most represents the majority of people in the country – a mix of economic interventionism, cultural conservatism and steady patriotism. Politicians and political candidates tend to fit neatly into political boxes, sharing every element of the beliefs of a political party. Voters don't fit so neatly into boxes.

This creates the 'paradox of the centre ground', where what is described as 'centrism' doesn't represent where most of the people are on the political spectrum and merely represents continuity of the modern political and economic settlement.

Pollster Matt Singh put this neatly when he talked about

the inaccuracy of the widespread assumption that the 'gap' in modern politics is in the liberal centre. That may be the perception among the commentariat and in the political Twittersphere – overwhelmingly pro-Remain – but neither of these bubbles is Britain

... The segment likeliest to feel unrepresented is the economically left-wing, socially conservative one – this group were two-and-a-half times likelier than the average person to think the politicians don't care what they think, and seven times likelier than liberal centrists. Fifty-five per cent of those that voted in 2017 backed Labour (although many have stopped voting) and three-quarters voted Leave in 2016 ... if we're going to talk about a gap in the pro-European liberal centre, we should keep in mind that there's a considerably bigger gap on the socially conservative left.

The centre ground is the equivalent of alchemy for many politicians. Most recently, The Independent Group, which became Change UK, launched with a proclaimed desire to reclaim the political centre ground. The failure of the party to win a single seat at the European elections in 2019 and their failure to even hit 1 per cent in subsequent opinion polls show that their belief that more metro-liberalism was the route to political success was over-egged. By contrast, the success of the Brexit Party is evidence that many voters still don't feel that their concerns are being addressed by mainstream politicians.

In truth, those who position themselves as being from the political centre are probably as far from the bulk of the population as those they posit to be at the extremes. Today's centrists are united by three elements: a belief that Brexit should be reversed or shouldn't happen at all; a belief in economic liberalism; and what can vaguely be described as the ideas of 'metropolitan liberalism'.

In each of these cases, the views of the population don't tend to be where politicians of the self-defined centre suggest they should be. There has been no complete reversal in the public view about Brexit. Equally, the British people don't share the belief in economic liberalism of the liberal centrists. They are much more likely to believe in some form of state intervention. Ivor Crewe famously showed how the British people had become less, not more, economically Thatcherite during her time in office, and there has been little wholehearted embrace of the liberal economic model in the decades since.

A poll in 2018, for example, found that only 27 per cent of all voters and just half of Tory voters agreed with the statement 'private enterprise is the best way to solve Britain's problems'. It should be noted that only 21 per cent disagreed with the statement, with most voters being indifferent. YouGov polling has also clearly shown that voters refuse to be placed in the easy categories beloved of politicians. In almost all cases, voters don't fall into the liberal centrist category. They found that 61 per cent of voters supported increasing the minimum wage to £10 an hour, 58 per cent supported widescale nationalisation, 52 per cent supported increased taxes on the rich and 51 per cent backed workers on boards. The same poll found that two thirds supported ending benefits for people who turn down job offers and 54 per cent favour a total ban on immigration for the next two years. The poll also showed that voters regarded terms like left- or right-wing to be meaningless, with only 18 per cent describing themselves as right-wing and 22 per cent as left-wing. More Tory voters described themselves as 'neither left- or right-wing' than as right-wing.

The astute political commentator Steve Richards has pointed out that much of the debate in modern British politics is dominated by a false understanding of the nature of the centre ground. As he has noted, positing Remain/Brexit as the foremost political dividing line in British politics leads to a fundamental misunderstanding of these dividing lines. For him, this is exemplified by BBC presenter Evan Davies suggesting that Polly Toynbee and George Osborne both had similar politics because of their views about Brexit. Davies argued that the dividing line is now between 'open' and 'closed', with Brexit being the fundamental embodiment of this. Richards argues that such a view is common at institutions like *The Times* and the BBC.

All too often the paradigm shift towards open/closed is used as an excuse to try to shut down important economic and social debates. The media articulation of centrism as being both 'moderate' and defined by economic and social liberalism is explicitly designed to frame those views as 'acceptable' and others as marginal or extreme. Ergo: open is good, closed is bad. The truth, however, is some distance from this comfortable narrative, which works for the powerful people who articulate it, but rather less for those people in forgotten towns and villages. To return to the words of Disraeli: 'Liberal opinions are very convenient opinions for the rich and powerful.' The difficulty in British politics isn't the absence of a party that is anti-Brexit, economically liberal and socially individualist. The Liberal Democrats were all of these things and failed to break out of single digits in the 2017 election.

As Goodhart has pointed out, there is a clear 'missing majority ... of lower-income, less well-educated people who remain significantly less liberal than the graduate Anywhere class but still prefer moderately social democratic economic ... policies and better protection from globalisation'. 'Centrism' might well be closer to the 'social patriotism' of early Blair, melding social democracy with a patriotism and a muscular approach to crime and defence, than to the neo-liberal consensus of latter Blair and early Cameron. There might be a gap in the market in British politics. It's just that the gap isn't where most commentators think it is. As I'll make clear later, the disregarded concept of One Nation represents the best way to ensure that these unrepresented opinions are heard again.

THE FALL OF POLITICAL PARTIES

Even with the Corbyn impact on Labour membership, political parties remain a tiny interest for a tiny part of the population – just over 1 per cent of the population are members of a political party, an obvious reason being that people who feel that politics has little to say to them feel disinclined to participate actively in it.

Tory Party membership has fallen from its heyday in the 1950s, when some academic surveys suggest that its membership was as high as 2.8 million, although it has recently recovered from a low point to be almost 200,000. Labour Party membership, after years of decline, was given a considerable, and unexpected, fillip with the rise of Jeremy Corbyn, with recent estimates putting the figure at between 400,000 and 500,000 – still well below the membership numbers of the 1950s and seemingly now back in decline. Contrast these figures with the National Trust

(4 million members), RSPCA (400,000 donors) and RSPB (over one million members), or even the more overtly political activism of Greenpeace or Friends of the Earth. Environmental groups between them have some 4.5 million members in the UK (it should be acknowledged that there might be some overlap).

Despite this historic decline in membership, members of political parties have more power now than they have ever had. It's one of the great ironies of modern politics that the rise in the power of party members has coincided almost exactly with the decline in their number.

Party members also have a great deal of power over the selection of MPs. Within Labour, more power has gone to a handful of trade unions and to national organisations with dogmatic aims, making it even less likely that the interests of disenchanted voters in forgotten towns will be adequately reflected.

There is considerable evidence that these powerful members are both more middle-class and more politically dogmatic than members of the public. Fascinating analysis from academic Tim Bale and his colleagues at Queen Mary's University has put this into perspective. They found that political party membership was overwhelmingly the preserve of the middle class – with 86 per cent of Tory members and 77 per cent of Labour members being middle class.

During the age of mass membership, organisations like the Primrose League helped to galvanise working-class Toryism – at one point it had more members than the British trade union movement. Conservative clubs also provided a social base for mass membership Toryism in an age when party membership was based on a loose, more social affiliation and a set of values, rather than a strict dogma.

Labour's growth in membership has also created a very different membership base to the working-class, town-based membership of the post-war period. Instead, according to internal party documentation, the majority of Labour's post-2015 members are 'high-status city dwellers'. The rise in internal party democracy has occurred at the same time as both major parties have become more middle class – further cementing the shift away from the interests and concerns of working-class voters based in towns.

The set-piece events in the political calendar – party conferences – might also accentuate this trend. They exist to bring together the party faithful, to act as a rallying cry and, possibly most importantly, to fill the coffers of political parties. These events do not, however, do anything to help ensure that politics meets the needs of those towns and those voters who have been long forgotten.

Politicians will generally work for weeks, or even months, on their party conference speeches. They know that a successful speech will increase their stock with both party leaders and the party faithful. The political media who will also follow the party conference circus will be likely to mark up politicians who 'wow' the conference – with a successful conference speech often leading to MPs being described as 'rising stars' or 'leadership contenders'.

Politicians are less likely to think that they should pitch their conference speeches to an audience beyond the hall. For one thing, television audiences for party conferences aren't going to challenge *Morecambe and Wise* in the record books, and a speech that is badly received in the conference hall is sure to attract the wrong kind of media attention. The goal of politicians is to inspire the party activists in their hall – which creates a perverse incentive to ignore the population at large while they do so. Through its very design, the political system has inadvertently made it less likely that voters in forgotten towns will have their voices heard or have a more substantial input in the political process.

Party politics has seen many backgrounds and opinions under-represented for too long. This tends to overestimate the metropolitan and underestimate those places that have long been ignored. This detachment is seen in the inability of many politicians to speak the language of the people (the popularity of politicians ranging from Ken Clarke to Boris Johnson lies in part in their authenticity and their ability to use everyday language). Only by ensuring that all voices are heard and respected will an effective political renewal be possible.

CHAPTER FOUR

THE BREAKING OF THE SOCIAL CONTRACT: A TRAGEDY IN THREE PARTS

Everybody knows that the dice are loaded.
Everybody rolls with their fingers crossed.
LEONARD COHEN, 'EVERYBODY KNOWS'

The coarsening of political discourse, the worrying emergence of echo chambers and the splintering into irreconcilable political tribes demonstrate that the threads holding us together are fraying at the edges. These threads, binding society and composed of mutual obligations and a feeling of national solidarity, are enormously important as part of a functioning and vibrant democracy. Key to this is a feeling of trust by the governed in those who govern them and, crucially, a sense that the government has the best interests of all of the people at heart. A vibrant democracy is one that accepts differences of opinion in good faith and is able to dispute those opinions without doubting the motives of people you disagree with. That is not the state of British democracy at the moment.

The Brexit vote and the response to it illustrated a country that was losing mutual respect and the ability to listen to different opinions. The use of the vote as an expression of protest against the economic and political settlement in many parts of the country, and particularly in the forgotten towns, suggested that many citizens no longer felt that the contract was delivering mutual benefits. For many, this feeling of trust has diminished almost to breaking point. This situation has been driven by many factors. Key among them must be deindustrialisation and its aftermath, the breach of trust that came with mass immigration and a misjudged war (both sold with either no consent or an inadequate prospectus), and a banking crash and its consequences that confirmed many people's worst fears about in whose interests the economy was run.

DEINDUSTRIALISATION AND A LOSS OF WORTH

Deindustrialisation has had a profound impact on the psyche and respect, as well as the economy, of many post-industrial towns. The argument that some form of deindustrialisation was inevitable is not without merit, particularly in the case of coal mining. The same cannot be said in the case of other industries, in which Germany, for example, continues to prosper. Manufacturing accounts for 10 per cent of the economy today, less than half that of Germany and a third of the level in South Korea, a country hallmarked by its high levels of innovation. The impact of deindustrialisation was also felt in the UK's research and development (R&D) base, with our private and public R&D spending being well below the OECD average, and in the loss of generations of skills and apprenticeship schemes. The decline in R&D post deindustrialisation also contributed to the unbalancing of the UK's economy, with the most recent figures showing that the south-east of England accounted for a huge 37 per cent of the total R&D spend in the UK.

The decline in manufacturing should be considered hand in hand with the UK's productivity crisis and the ongoing regional divide. Manufacturing is more productive than any other sector of the economy, and a carelessness around the deindustrialisation of recent decades means that the UK has deindustrialised more than any other G20 economy. As Neil O'Brien argues, tackling this long-running productivity problem would 'transform our living standards and our ability to pay for public services'.

An ONS release earlier in 2019 also put the regional productivity divide in context, pointing out that the only other region with productivity above the UK average was the south-east, with productivity 8 per cent above the UK average.

> In Wales and Northern Ireland, productivity was 16 to 17 per cent below the UK average. The regions of the north of England and the midlands (the North East, the North West, Yorkshire and the Humber, the East Midlands and the West Midlands) had productivity levels between 7 per cent and 15 per cent below the UK average.

Nick Timothy has highlighted that this productivity divide is also hamstrung by divides in public investment, with Oxford, Cambridge and London between them accounting for almost half of the entire public R&D investment.

In the 1970s and 1980s, Britain was told that it could no longer make things and that it should rely almost purely on the service sector. This was a false idea. The truth is that British industry needed innovation, investment and modernisation. Poor management practices and diabolical industrial relations (particularly following the capture of the trade unions by the hard left) dealt self-inflicted and unforgivable blows to British industry. Nationalisation was another self-inflicted wound, leaving many industries at the whim of politicians and often starving them of both investment and necessary private-sector discipline. That was all compounded by an ill-judged flirtation with monetarism at a time when British industry was at its weakest, which resulted in a quarter of manufacturing capacity being lost in two years.

This, of course, followed years of under-investment, union militancy and poor management. It's folly to blame the decline of manufacturing on one government; it was a process that had, sadly, been happening for many years. It would be remiss, however, to ignore the fact that a brief monetarist experiment in the early 1980s certainly didn't do anything to improve the situation. It should be acknowledged that a 'shake out', where heavy industry declined and services increased as a share of the economy, occurred across the developed world. But it happened with a greater severity in the UK than in any other major economy, and this has impacted our productivity and living standards. As I set out later, government should be ambitious in reversing this trend and pushing for a high-skill, high-tech reindustrialisation of long-declining regions.

The social impact of deindustrialisation is something that diminished the social fabric, with the highest levels of 'worklessness' being in towns that were dependent on heavy industry. That this is still the situation in towns that lost their industry over three or four decades ago shows how substantial the impact was and how little was done to cushion it.

When David Cameron talked about a broken society, he failed to acknowledge adequately that much of it had been broken in the 1980s and 1990s. Deindustrialisation didn't, of course, start with the Thatcher government (most of the Durham coalfield was closed by the 1970s and Harold Wilson closed more pits than Margaret Thatcher). There were 1,570 deep coal mines in 1945. By 1964, there were 565 deep mines managed by the National Coal Board (NCB), which fell to 293 by 1970 and 219 by 1979. Employment figures tell a similar story, with employment in coal mining falling from 700,000 in 1945 to 502,000 in 1964 to 290,000 in 1970. The story of an industry destroyed by callous Tories, therefore, just isn't true.

Arguments about statistics aside, the truth is that in many coal mining areas, the 1970s and '80s stand as the decades during which communities fell into neglect. The issue wasn't the loss of industry per se, but the signal failure to replace it adequately. These areas have, to adopt the lexicon, been 'left behind', with a myriad of social and economic consequences. As we have already discussed, in too many cases, high-value, high-skill, relatively high-wage occupations in which people rightly took pride were 'replaced' with low-skill, low-wage occupations. This was difficult for the individuals involved but also for the national economy: high-skill jobs are much more likely to boost productivity as a whole. What could and should have been focused retraining efforts, in order to help towns move from one industry to the next, were instead token and piecemeal. They were certainly no match to the innovative retraining offered to workers in Germany, through the Employment or Conversion Plans.

Lord (Norman) Tebbit – by no means a limp leftist – has admitted that the impact of the pit closures was far-reaching. In an interview to mark the twentieth anniversary of the miners' strike, he said:

> Many of these [mining] communities were completely devastated, with people out of work turning to drugs and no real man's work because all the jobs had gone. There is no doubt that this led to a breakdown in these communities with families breaking up and youths going out of control. The scale of the closures went too far. The damage done to those communities was enormous as a result of the strike.

What this means for the social contract is abundantly clear. For many, deindustrialisation and its aftermath meant that they believed that their livelihoods were regarded as less valid than others in the country and that their voice was less important. Whether this is true or not, it is how many people felt. They believed that their concerns had become marginal for politicians and their economic pain was somehow seen as legitimate collateral damage. This was captured for dramatic effect and with some theatrical licence in films such as *Brassed Off* and *The Full Monty*. In *Brassed Off*, about a colliery band from a pit village that loses its colliery, the band leader, played by Pete Postlethwaite, gives an impassioned speech rejecting an award given to the brass band. He complained about the systematic destruction of 'an entire industry':

And not just our industry – our communities, our homes, our lives … [When the colliery closed] another thousand men lost their jobs. And that's not all they lost. Most of them lost the will to win a while ago. A few of them even lost the will to fight. But when it comes to losing the will to live, to breathe, the point is: if this lot were seals or whales, you'd all be up in bloody arms. But they're not, are they? No, no, they're not. They're just ordinary common-or-garden honest, decent human beings. And not one of them with an ounce of bloody hope left.

Little wonder that, decades later, the same marginalised communities rallied behind a banner that gave them the option of 'taking back control'. They had been told for decades that their voice was irrelevant, that global economic forces and immovable economic rules had made democratic control a mirage and democratic decision-making effectively irrelevant. Who can be surprised that when presented with an opportunity to 'take back control', all but one of the former coalfields and almost all of the 'post-industrial' towns grabbed that opportunity?

CHANGE WITHOUT CONSENT? THE IMPACT OF UNCONTROLLED IMMIGRATION ON FORGOTTEN TOWNS

The impact of the mass immigration that started with the accession of new EU members in 2004 was, in the words of a demographic expert, 'historically unprecedented'. This influx of new workers was one of the biggest, and least expected, influxes of people in British history. Between May 2004 and June 2006, 427,000 workers from eight EU accession countries applied successfully for work in the UK, and this figure is more likely to be above 600,000 if self-employed workers, such as builders, are included. Other estimates put the figure at over a million a year. By 2016, the figure had grown to 2 million. Before accession, government ministers predicted that this figure would be no more than 15,000 a year. Ed Balls, who was an adviser to the Chancellor at the time, now says, 'We didn't see the extent to which low-wage people would move.'

There's little doubt that the immigration brought some economic benefits. Employers in particular benefited, but low-paid workers less so, with evidence showing that the weight of mass immigration put pressure on wages at the lower end of the income spectrum. As the now-public conversations between Lord King and Tony Blair illustrate, a primary reason for encouraging such an unprecedented surge in immigration was to keep wages down, with recently released papers showing that then Bank of England Governor, Lord King, pressed the case 'to open the labour market without transition on the grounds that it would help lower wage growth'.

A study by University College London, for example, found that immigration had a negative impact on the lowest-paid 5 per cent of the labour market and a positive impact for the highest paid. Even former Labour leader Ed Miliband was to acknowledge that his party had 'got it wrong' on immigration and that this had impacted wages at the lower end of the wage scale.

In viewing it through a purely economic prism, Blairites shared the laissez-faire tendency of regarding the market nexus as the sole parameter for decision-making. It also meant that British firms, with a ready supply of already skilled labour, had no real incentive to invest in training home-grown workers or building high-quality apprenticeship schemes. Why would a company train a young British worker if somebody from eastern Europe was able to do the same job, for the same wage as a trainee, and already had the requisite skills? This had a knock-on impact on those towns that already struggled with low levels of skills.

Mass immigration changed the nature of many communities almost overnight, in a way that those communities hadn't been led to expect or in any way consulted over. Such a change was in no party manifesto and happened without any real debate. For many voters, this stopped being government by consent, with cultural loss and change being more important than economic benefit.

As I've mentioned, the economic benefit was less likely to be felt further down the social scale. Jon Cruddas MP represents Dagenham, a town that saw massive immigration and tremendous economic disruption simultaneously. As he said in an interview in 2010:

> The issue of immigration has been so significant in Barking and Dagenham because it is seen to have ruptured a tacit covenant between the traditional working class and Labour – a covenant about housing, work, employment, a sense of neighbourliness and community ... the massive changes to the community eroded people's sense of duty and obligation ... But go back to the fundamental

questions here, which is what is this immigration debate about? Obviously, a lot of it is driven by the velocity of change and a sense of bewilderment and the loss and hopelessness that goes with it. And this is part of a deeper breach of a tacit covenant with the community here with Labour. How do we rebuild it?

Here, Cruddas hits upon a key point about the debate about immigration under New Labour. As with many issues, it was portrayed as an issue of an improved *national* economy and an engagement in an *international* community, based on what was best for big business. It didn't consider the impact on the local community, or the impact on areas where competition for low-paid, low-skilled work was strongest.

Actively encouraging mass immigration also changed the social contract in another, more subtle, but still important, way. Nation states, and their supporting welfare state, require at least a degree of sympathy between citizens, a degree of mutual understanding and a shared sense of belonging. In short, people need to think that they have enough commonality and sense of belonging with their fellow citizens to be willing to allow their taxes to help them in times of need. Other elements that chipped away at the social contract have, of course, also chipped away at this sense, but large-scale mass immigration, encouraged for economic reasons, has also diminished this sense of solidarity. David Sinclair, in his controversial but important book *Strangers in Our Midst*, suggests that the ability to control borders based on domestic political priorities is an important element of national self-determination. He argues that an 'open doors' approach to immigration would effectively diminish this and with it the solidarity needed in a functioning democracy.

The point about both the free rein given to the City of London and the large-scale immigration from eastern Europe is that both were done *to*, not *with*, the people. There was no public discussion about large-scale immigration, nor was there ever widescale public acceptance that the economy should have been tilted in favour of the City of London. Both created a feeling that the thoughts and wishes of the bulk of the nation weren't being considered in some elements of policy-making. And it would lead to particular grievance when the economy crashed.

A YouGov poll taken at the end of Blair's premiership found that the failure to control immigration was regarded as his biggest in office – a stark indication that he had failed to achieve anything close to public consent on the issue. For a premiership that had started with such communitarian hope of a restored social contract, it was particularly damaging that the impact of Iraq and mass immigration in particular was to leave that contract more weakened than ever. The expenses scandal that followed Blair further diminished trust in Parliament and other institutions. But it was the banking crash and the deep cuts that were implemented as a result that, for many, finally broke their trust in the political and economic system.

THE BANKING CRASH – AND WHAT CAME NEXT

Already, before 2008, whole communities in places like Consett felt that the actions of politicians brought little real benefit to them and that decisions weren't being made with their interests in mind. The 2008 banking crisis, its aftermath and how it was handled by politicians and central bankers helped to turn this rift into a crisis of confidence as people compared the devastating impact of the financial crash on England's forgotten towns with the minimal impact on those who had caused the crisis in the first place.

All governments since 1979 (and arguably 1976) had been heavily deregulatory, and this was no more the case than in financial services. In successive Mansion House speeches, Gordon Brown boasted of the 'light touch' approach to financial regulation. He even suggested in 2007 that history 'will record [this era] as the beginning of a new golden age for the City of London' and that 'in the first decades of the twenty-first century ... a new world order was created'. This was clearly an 'order' that didn't bring a great deal of benefit to towns like Barnsley and Consett. He went into more detail about this philosophy in 2005 in his 'Better Regulation Action Plan':

> In a risk based approach there is no inspection without justification, no form filling without justification, and no information requirements without justification. Not just a light touch but a limited touch. Instead of routine regulation attempting to cover all, we adopt a risk based approach which targets only the necessary few.
>
> A risk based approach helps move us a million miles away from the old assumption – the assumption since the first legislation of Victorian times – that business, unregulated, will invariably act irresponsibly. The better view is that businesses want to act

responsibly. Reputation with customers and investors is more important to behaviour than regulation, and transparency – backed up by the light touch – can be more effective than the heavy hand.

Needless to say, this drew heavily on the laissez-faire belief that regulation itself was an evil and the only role of the state was to 'get out of the way'.

If anything, the upper echelons of the Tory Party during Blair's premiership were criticising Brown for regulating the banks too much, rather than too little. Only two years before the financial crisis, the recently elected Tory leader David Cameron made a speech in which he saluted the City of London as a 'great UK success story', with 'low regulation' being a key part in that success. In 2006, the then shadow Chancellor George Osborne was worrying that much of the regulation introduced to the City of London 'has been burdensome, complex and makes cross-border market penetration more difficult'.

Cameron was speaking for a whole generation of politicians when he argued, only days before the most catastrophic financial collapse since the Great Depression:

[The] debate is now settled. Over the past fifteen years, governments across the world have put into practice the principles of monetary discipline and free enterprise. The result? A vast increase in global wealth. The world economy more stable than for a generation ... I'm proud that this is one of the few countries in the world where all serious candidates for high office support the principles of free trade and monetary discipline.

In fact, a 'new world order' and a 'global success story' had left the UK economically and regionally imbalanced, with wealth concentrated in the City of London and away from the once-mighty industrial towns. The City of London now has a Gross Value Added (GVA) per head of over £300,000, compared to a national average of only £26,000 (it is as low as £16,000 in County Durham). This reflected the failure to help towns recover from decline of industry, but also the concentration of lending power and wealth in just one part of the country. Despite these clear disparities, the debate was presumed to be settled, with the discontents of globalisation being regarded as left-wing mavericks or the last remnants of a romantic Toryism.

The dominance of financial services and years spent neglecting manufacturing and building a stronger productive base meant that the British economy was dangerously exposed when the crisis hit the financial sector in 2008 and the myth of the self-regulating market was laid bare. Once again, consumer spending growth was almost wholly funded by access to cheap credit, rather than wage growth or improved productivity. This, along with the shrinking share of the economy devoted to manufacturing, meant that the UK was hit much harder than many economies, such as Germany, by the severe impact of the financial crisis.

The banking crisis was caused by one thing: the behaviour of bankers and the desire to make a quick buck. It saw building societies, once entrenched in their communities, transformed into banks who were as reckless as any other. Banks around the world became guilty of 'overleveraging', in effect borrowing more than they would ever be capable of paying back based on the assumption that the financial good times would last for ever. Although the recession indisputably started on Wall Street, it was Main Street, particularly in our towns, that suffered the most. It was the political and economic response to this that marked the beginning of both a missed opportunity and a populist revolt.

MAIN STREET LOSING OUT AGAIN: THE POLITICAL RESPONSE TO THE BANKING CRASH

Although Brown and Darling's response to the crisis had much to commend it, they failed to deliver any lasting international change. The Depression and Second World War had led the 'Never Again' politicians and economists of the 1940s to deliver a Bretton Woods agreement designed to ensure that such a collapse wouldn't be repeated and to tame some of what Keynes described as the 'animal spirits' who had caused the crash in the first place. There was no equivalent of Bretton Woods in the twenty-first century.

Northern Rock is symbolic of the decline of once-important community institutions and of the further damage that the crash caused to our towns. Northern Rock, for some time, was illustrated as an example of the economic resurgence in the north-east and was a major employer for the area's suburbs in particular, so the demise of the bank had a devastating economic and psychological impact. As the *Financial Times* commented on the tenth anniversary of the bank's decline:

Pride in Northern Rock – its very name evoking solidity – had engendered huge loyalty. The Newcastle-based bank's collapse in September 2007 and the treatment of its shareholders – many of them local people whose investments were rendered worthless when the company was nationalised six months later – have left a bitter taste in the region. There is also a lingering sense that the company was a victim: it was, think some locals, a northern company that got the rough end of the southern stick.

Northern Rock turned from a community-embedded building society to a bank that became catastrophically overleveraged and its collapse was one of the first signs of the severity of the crash. One of the architects of its demise is now a prominent advocate for the kind of ultra-free-market ideas that led Northern Rock crashing to the ground.

The banking crisis also accentuated the regional inequalities that have blighted the country for over a century. For example, GDP for London and the south-east had recovered to 2008 levels within two years, whereas in some parts of the country, such as the north-east, this recovery had still not happened a decade later. The major lasting impact was on wages and cost of living that remains to this day.

The dominance of finance has been a fundamental part of the trampling of the social contract. While the City of London, contributing 2.4 per cent to the national income, is among the richest land pockets in the world, two of the most abjectly poor boroughs lie on its doorstep. The strength of the City might be felt in the pages of 'How to Spend It' or in the Porsche dealerships nearby, but this certainly doesn't translate to towns like Barnsley, Doncaster or Consett.

The banking crash produced devastating consequences for the great bulk of the population. Indeed, to many it seems the only people who *haven't* seen dire consequences are those within the banking industry itself – those whose reckless behaviour caused economic stagnation and insecurity for the bulk of society and those who caused the financial crash in the first place. This lack of apparent remorse and punishment has contributed greatly to anger throughout Britain.

The initial shock of the banking crash was substantial and severe. Familiar names on Britain's high streets such as Woolworths disappeared, leaving our forgotten towns in an even more troubled state than they were in before 2008. GDP reduced by 6 per cent between the first quarter of 2008 and the second quarter of 2009. It took the UK economy five years to recover that lost GDP and the north even longer. Unemployment shot up, with the rate increasing from 5.3 per cent in 2008 to a high of 8.1 per cent in 2011. Earnings consistently lagged behind prices for most of the decade following the crisis, meaning that people were effectively poorer in real terms. People in towns saw that lasting economic damage around them and also noticed that bankers still seemed to be doing very well despite the crash that their behaviour had caused.

President Roosevelt's first inaugural address is famous for the disdain in which he held those who had caused the devastating crisis and the 'do nothing' economic philosophy of his predecessors, which had served to make the crisis worse. His 1933 speech celebrating the fact that the 'money lenders have fled from their high seats in the temple of our civilisation' had no equivalent in the post-2008 environment. Nor did his second inaugural address, where he declared that 'Government by organised money is just as dangerous as government by organised mob.'

As we've mentioned, after the Great Depression, governments took great steps to ensure that such an event could not be repeated. They also made substantial moves to ensure that those who caused the crash were held responsible for it. There was no such reckoning after 2008, with Iceland being the only country to respond with equal severity.

The centralisation of finance in the City of London is both a great strength and a great weakness for the UK. It has powered London towards becoming the most prosperous area in northern Europe and London is generally regarded as the global centre for finance. But as we have seen, this has a potentially destabilising influence on the remainder of the economy, with sectors other than finance being regarded as 'second-tier', and is geographically tilted towards the south-east of England. The City also wields enormous political muscle as a result, meaning that policies of all parties have tended to favour it in recent decades.

It has also had the impact of de-rooting finance and starving productive industry, particularly in the regions, of the investment that industry needs to modernise, compete and be more productive. The building societies that once served to link capital directly with communities have been torn up in a short-termist march to profit. As I'll set out later, there's a real need to address this, and tackling the centralisation of finance must be as much of a priority as restoring a sense of sanity and balance to our politics.

Overall, there is a strong and growing feeling that those responsible for the banking crash aren't those who have suffered from it. The bankers themselves remain highly paid and immune from the rest of the country's struggles. For the bulk of the population, the years since the banking crash have been marked by stagnation. People are angry and they are right to be.

AUSTERITY AND THE SOCIAL CONTRACT – 'IT'S COMPLICATED'

The debate about austerity in the years following the banking crash is a complicated one. There's little doubt that the UK's structural deficit had grown too large and, if left untouched, would have caused ongoing damage to the economy and the UK's ability to fund public services over the longer term. Getting the public finances back under control was essential for any programme of national reconstruction, including of the kind recommended in this book, which would have been impossible with out-of-control public finances. Measures taken to tackle an unsustainable deficit mean that our freedom of manoeuvre is now greater than it would have been if the deficit was allowed to carry on ballooning. This means that debt is now relatively cheap, and spending can be boosted in order to deliver the kind of revolutionary investment in infrastructure and skills that I make the case for in this book.

The simple-headed 'austerity bad, public spending good' narrative pushed by some on the hard left is wide of the mark – national bankruptcy doesn't equate to a New Jerusalem, as Stafford Cripps very much understood. Some kind of action to tackle the deficit achieved considerable support, particularly when it was regarded as an action to tackle a known and identified problem.

That shouldn't take away from the fact that the perception of austerity was something that disproportionately impacted towns that were already suffering from decades of failures to properly address the problems that flowed from deindustrialisation. Levels of 'worklessness' were higher in these post-industrial towns, meaning that benefit cuts hit them disproportionately hard. The proportion of people in work who depend on in-work benefits is also higher in these areas, meaning that they were hit harder by the ongoing benefit freeze. Publicly funded projects that helped to provide a focal point for community life, such as community centres, Sure Start centres and even youth clubs, found that they had their money supply limited. The impact on shared community space and the upkeep of the shared public realm was also noticeable.

Recent decades have led to a growing perception that the needs of many towns and many voters are regularly ignored. These voters, as we noted earlier, lack a sense of agency and control and have been gradually disengaged from an economic and political settlement that they no longer feel works for them. Before considering how to remake this settlement and renew the social contract, we should consider the political and economic developments that ultimately resulted in division and disenchantment.

CHAPTER FIVE

THE LIMITS OF THE MARKET: THE CREATION OF AN ATOMISED COUNTRY?

Liberal opinions are very convenient opinions
for the rich and powerful.
— BENJAMIN DISRAELI

There was indeed a considerable shouting about what they called
Conservative principles; but the awkward question naturally
arose, what will you conserve?
— BENJAMIN DISRAELI, *CONINGSBY*

The story of recent decades is a story of how economic liberalism (or even libertarianism) and identity liberalism have grown dominant in public policy and ideas. Both arose for good reasons and to tackle real and important problems. Both, however, evolved from being pragmatic responses to known issues to hardened dogmas that created new problems in themselves. A growing dependence on economic and identity liberalism has done little to tackle the issues that have led to people in the forgotten towns feeling – and being – 'left behind'. Here I make the case for a more nuanced approach, which doesn't remove the gains that have been achieved, but is more inclusive and less dogmatic.

MARKET LIBERALISM THEN AND NOW

Margaret Thatcher is clearly the dominant individual of the politics of recent decades. She opened up the UK economy and utterly transformed the conversation about the role and nature of the state. In many ways, she was a political revolutionary, and she laid the groundwork for the politics and economics that continue to dominate. She strengthened the nation state in many ways, while at the same time weakening it in many practical terms. The Tory Party was boosted electorally during her time in office, but instilling it with a rigid dogma left it also more exposed in later years with a reduced ability to adapt to changing circumstances.

In the late 1970s and early 1980s, as I'll set out, rolling back the state and boosting entrepreneurialism was a national priority. The state was too large and enterprise too hamstrung. This was, in many ways, a very Tory response to address known problems, to restore balance where the state had grown too large and the market too small, and to help share property rights more widely. Where this pragmatic response later hardened into a dogma, however, it seemed to suggest that all the state had to do was 'get out of the way', and it had little to add when a reduction in state activity didn't see economic revival in forgotten towns. This meant that a post-Thatcher Toryism became more and more economically determinist and began to lack an overriding and compelling governing philosophy. In too many cases, the economically libertarian strain of Conservatism began to lack ideas beyond 'rolling back the state', even when it became clear that a smaller state wasn't enough in itself to tackle deep-seated social and economic issues. Thatcherism created a myth from which it has proven difficult for the Conservatives to escape, despite the fact that the challenges she faced are very different to the challenges the country faces today. That is not to belittle the benefits that flowed from changes made in the late 1970s and 1980s; more to say that a different set of problems needs a different set of solutions.

Politicians held to the central nostrums of laissez-faire even after the concept of self-regulating markets had been tested to destruction by the 2008 banking crash, when the global economy was resettled purely by government action. The crash brought to mind the words of Karl Polanyi in *The Great Transformation*: 'The most recent global financial crisis reminded the current generation of the lessons that their grandparents had learned in the Great Depression: the self-regulating economy does not always work as well as its proponents would like us to believe.'

The continuity of British politics around the laissez-faire model is well summarised by the excellent *Thatcher and Sons*, written by Simon Jenkins when Gordon Brown was in Downing Street. Little changed when Cameron, Osborne and Clegg were at the helm of government and, as Steve Richards has observed, even Cameron's declaration that 'there is such a thing as society, it's just not the same as the state' was a repackaging of Thatcherism, rather than its repudiation.

Theresa May, with her 'burning injustices' speech, and Boris Johnson, with his acknowledgement that 'for too long politicians have failed to deliver on what is needed', show that there is now a greater understanding within the Tory Party than for decades that the economic settlement hasn't worked for many people. This followed a period of soul-searching after the Brexit referendum when many politicians and opinion formers acknowledged that a settlement that merely depends on the state getting out of the way isn't one that is working for many millions of people, and that using the state where necessary is both popular and the right thing to do. There is a growing understanding that, in the words of impressive Tory moderniser Rob Halfon, 'Thatcherism is not enough' and Conservatism needs to take social justice as seriously as it takes a strong economy.

WHY LAISSEZ-FAIRE RE-EMERGED

It was Disraeli's Tory governments that signalled an end to the laissez-faire liberalism of the Whigs and, later, the Liberals. In the period between then and the 1970s, the balance between state and market altered, but there was little appetite to return to a world where the self-correcting market ruled supreme. At this point, however, the ideas of Mises and, in particular, Hayek became popular again.

Runaway inflation, over-powerful trade unions, a state that had grown too large and a virtually ungovernable country meant that economic liberals, such as Friedman in the US and Minford in the UK, could remake the argument for a revived laissez-faire. In many cases, they had a point. It was crucial that economic reform was achieved so that the UK could cease to be the 'sick man of Europe'. Many of these reforms were pragmatic responses to known problems.

As economist and historian Lord Skidelsky has argued, the post-war 'consensus' phase has two distinct instalments. The first, from 1940 until around 1964, was largely successful, despite a fetish for nationalisation, which failed British industry and squeezed out necessary investment. The second period, from 1964 to 1979, was marked by repeated failure and something close to a national nervous breakdown. Successive governments misused Keynesian economics and indulged in a haphazard and increasingly idiotic 'stop-go' approach to the economy as they pursued growth targets. This led to inflationary pressures, which fuelled increasing wage demands.

What became known as Thatcherism represented a response to this unique set of circumstances in the 1970s in the UK and, undoubtedly, it did a great deal of necessary work to tackle clear weaknesses. Private enterprise wasn't strong enough in pre-Thatcher Britain and unions held too much power, which they often used in a deeply irresponsible way – especially after the trade unions were hijacked by the hard left. British business didn't invest enough, labour markets were creaky and inflexible, and nationalisation had made the problem of lack of investment and old-fashioned business practices even worse. The country had become dangerously imbalanced in favour of trade union leaders who were seemingly incapable of using their power wisely or with any concern for the common good. Too few people owned their own homes or owned shares – the state owned far too much and business and private citizens owned far too little. The concept of national decline had been taken as a statement of fact and the country had become, in some ways, almost ungovernable.

By the end of Thatcher's time in power, controversies remained, but nobody would have described Britain as ungovernable, and our economy, particularly in the prosperous south-east, had become relatively successful by European terms. Victory in the Falklands War arrested the myth of national decline and restored a sense of national pride. Productivity increased across the economy and privatisation allowed a temporary broadening of share ownership, although this, sadly, could not be sustained. Similarly, Right to Buy allowed hundreds of thousands to buy their own home. Crippling rates of personal taxation were reduced, and Britain had a much more entrepreneurial culture. Trade unions were no longer in a position to act as a powerful vested interest or to bring the country to a halt on a whim. Thatcher's leadership was strong, her faith in the UK was unwavering, and many other countries, rather than seeing us as the 'sick man', actually started looking to us as a model to copy again.

All of these factors are overwhelmingly positive. It might be true that Thatcher merely accelerated global trends that were already clear, and that Callaghan instituted a shift in economic policy in 1976, but it was Thatcher's government that pushed these changes forward and made them into a new political and economic consensus.

As time wore on what started as a pragmatic response hardened into a dogma that became fearful of the impact of any state intervention in the market whatsoever. The philosophy prescribed an unrealistic wickedness to the state at all levels and an equally ideological, almost mystical, power to the unfettered free market, which often failed to live up to these vaulted expectations. To the most dogmatic of the economic libertarians, there was no question that didn't have the answer of the state 'getting out of the way', and no problem that the state couldn't make worse. In many ways, some conservatives had moved from being empirical to being dogmatic. Conservative abolition of Wages Councils and subsequent opposition to the minimum wage in the 1990s was an example of where free-market dogma had become all-consuming.

Whereas the limit of the state was the key argument in the 1970s, now the limit of markets is of equal relevance. There is no real laissez-faire response to the crisis of low wages, low productivity and low skills in many of our towns, and no laissez-faire response to the shortage of infrastructure that is holding many communities back. Laissez-faire alone cannot possibly respond to the challenge posed by rapid economic change, particularly given the important condition that individuals are not as flexible or moveable and communities not as malleable as ideology would have us believe.

THE CULTURAL CONTRADICTIONS OF THATCHERISM? LAISSEZ-FAIRE AND CONSERVATISM

As Shirley Letwin, one of the most influential Thatcherite thinkers, put it, Thatcherism was by no means purely an economic philosophy. In her *Anatomy of Thatcherism*, she made clear that it was also based on 'social and moral virtues'. Despite this, one of the enduring impacts of the rebirth of economic liberalism was to launch a programme of social change and cultural transformation that was utterly unintended, but equally permanent. Thatcherism may have been launched on the rhetoric of social and cultural conservatism, but many of the consequences of economic liberalism were anything but conservative. This would come as no surprise to the economic and social philosophers that the laissez-faire liberals often drew upon for inspiration, who perceived the power of the market precisely in its ability to be dynamic and to reshape. These are not values generally regarded as conservative.

These dynamics were noted by sociologist Daniel Bell in his 1970s classic, *The Cultural Contradictions of Capitalism*. He pointed out that capitalism, while being dependent on a strong work ethic, also had the consequence of giving rise to a culture that was both hedonistic and based on instant gratification. To this could be added a sense that the economic liberalism that has taken root in recent decades has over-emphasised individual whims at the expense of the collective and the wider community. The end result of this has been a broader social atomisation.

One of the most perceptive critics of the contradictions at the heart of laissez-faire liberalism and the attempt to shape it into a 'conservative' project is John Gray, a one-time believer in the 'new right' project, who has become one of the most compelling modern British philosophers. In the mid-1990s, he produced a paper suggesting that the increased dogmatism of free market economics had effectively destroyed the traditional Conservative project:

As she put it in an interview in 1981, 'Economics are the method: the object is to change the soul.' She succeeded in her object, though not in the way she wanted ... The bourgeois life of the 1950s – an idealised image of which she aimed to re-create: a middle-class world of secure livelihoods, dutiful families, and prudent saving for the future – has vanished without trace, along with the working-class communities that underpinned British industry. Dreaming of restoring a country that she believed was in danger of being lost, Thatcher brought into being one she could not have conceived.

For Gray, the impact of renewed laissez-faire was in many ways unconservative. As Rob Halfon argues, whereas Thatcherism had seen the importance of reducing the role of the state in national life, it didn't do enough to encourage a growth in social capital or a belief in social justice for those individuals or communities who were 'left behind'.

Whereas a resurgent economic liberalism delivered a much-needed boost to the economy, it didn't foresee that viewing the market nexus as the sole or primary basis of decision-making would weaken many of the other institutions that conservatives had traditionally held dear. In many areas, this means growing atomisation and a splintering of community institutions, a weakening of the family and its bonds, and a diminution of social structures.

This is illustrated by a number of datasets. The number of divorces, for example, rose from 138,000 in 1979 to 165,000 in 1993. The number of marriages also decreased markedly from 351,000 in 1981 to 306,000 in 1991, and that trend continued; by 2005 it was as low as 239,000. In 1979, only 12.5 per cent of babies were born outside marriage; by 1991, that number had gone up to 29.8 per cent.

Community institutions also witnesses a stark decline during this period, as well as the inevitable drop in the number of social, cricket and football clubs that were often subsidised by steelworks and coal mines. Pubs and Post Offices were two community hubs that saw a steep fall in their numbers. The Post Office network, for example, has reduced from over 22,000 branches in 1979 to around half that number today. Pubs are closing at rate of eighteen a week and 25 per cent have closed since 2001. Attendance at Anglican churches continues to decline and affiliation with the Church of England was at a record low in 2018, at 14 per cent – down to 2 per cent among young adults. Non-conformist churches, which played such a central role in community life, particularly in industrial areas, have seen their numbers plummet. These institutions aren't just important in their own right; they also represent important places for communities to come together and, in some areas, represent one of the only forces against atomisation.

One of the community institutions that had the steepest decline in numbers – and with it the most far-reaching consequences – was the building society. Building societies were predominantly local institutions, which encouraged saving and used to be a primary choice of lender for local people. The fact that they had to lend against existing security (at least until legislative changes in the 1980s) made them predominantly conservative bodies, with real community links. In 1980, some 78 per cent of new loans came from building societies.

In 1986, the government legislated to allow building societies to be taken over by banks, thus beginning the gradual diminution of an important community institution, which, as I've said, often had strong links to local businesses. In 1975, there were 385 building societies; in 1980, they had almost 6,000 branches and 5.3 million borrowers in the UK. By 1990, the number of societies had dramatically reduced to only 100. The most recent figures suggest that there are only forty-four building societies in the UK today, with fewer than 1,500 branches.

It's clear that the impact of economic liberalism has been that people are spending more time at work and less time with their families and in their communities. Many commentators have also attributed this development as 'post-Fordism', developed, perhaps unexpectedly, by a variety of commentators at *Marxism Today*. As John Harris recounts:

> The magazine's writers described the changes wrought by a new reality of small economic units, franchising, outsourcing, self-employment and part-time work – most of it driven by companies and corporations with a global reach – which they called 'Post-Fordism' ... Economies were becoming more fragmented and unpredictable, as the bureaucratic, top-down structures that had defined the first two-thirds of the twentieth century were pushed aside ... The conversations at Wortley Hall ... highlighted huge changes to the fabric of everyday life ... the increasing expectation of personal autonomy – and how seemingly unstoppable forces were weakening the traditional nation state.

It might be argued that such 'post-Fordism' was more relevant in those countries that had decided to become post-industrial, such as the UK, than those, such as Germany and Japan, who maintained the importance of manufacturing in their economic system. Nevertheless, these economic changes and the emphasis on 'personal autonomy' changed communitarian workplaces into much more atomised ones, with a broader societal impact.

Indeed, a 2007 poll said that nine out of ten people felt that communities were breaking down. Another poll found that people regarded the loss of local amenities as important factors in the breakdown of community spirit. A 2016 survey also showed that younger people were much less likely to know their neighbour or to check on their neighbour than older people; ONS data has shown that around 2.4 million people are suffering from 'chronic loneliness' – a trend at least partially linked to a breakdown in communities.

Researchers from the University of Sheffield found that

> the weakest communities in 1971 were stronger than the strongest communities in 2001. An astonishing 97 per cent of neighbourhoods had experienced this increased isolation over these thirty years ... The researchers conclude that the increase in anomie weakens the 'social glue' of communities. The result, they suggest, is that neighbourhoods are likely to be less trusting and more fearful.

This is, of course, not unique to the UK. American historian Marc Dunkelman talks about the decline of neighbourliness in the US and what he calls 'The Vanishing Neighbour'. He suggests that people may have what he calls 'inner ring' relationships with close family and friends, but recent years have led to a decline in community engagement and involvement in what he describes as the 'middle ring' of community organisations.

Community activity is far less likely in a society which either encourages long hours in some professions or, in some low-paid jobs, leaves people very little alternative to working long hours in multiple jobs. Similarly, key community institutions, such as churches, pubs and tightly knit workplaces, have declined just as other forces encouraging individualism have increased.

'A PREPAREDNESS TO LET CHANGE RUN ITS COURSE'

The revival of economic liberalism had two elements: the first diminishing the power of the state and 'unleashing' the power of the market; the second was to strengthen the nation state.

Few would have denied that some kind of economic change was necessary. The sheer speed of this transformation and the harsh impact on communities and institutions, especially when the communal impact was understood but regarded as secondary to economic dynamism, were, in many ways, fundamentally unconservative. It is now abundantly clear that answers that went beyond greater marketisation were necessary when a rolling back of the state had failed to create growth and dynamism for many towns and communities. A hardening of ideology meant that measures weren't taken that would have strengthened social capital and tackled issues faced by those who hadn't benefited from revolutionary economic changes.

Observers as diverse as Polanyi, Marx and Hayek have acknowledged that, left unchecked, market forces are destructive to communities and settled ways of life. The very essence of markets is that they are dynamic forces, with little respect for cultural traditions. As will be discussed later, a fundamental idea of traditional conservatism is that markets are essential to create wealth, but they must be moored within cultural norms and institutions. Conservatives are, thus, suspicious of markets that are unfettered and have no institutional or cultural underpinning.

This was one of Hayek's reasons for proclaiming that he was not a conservative. In the essay of the same name, he reminded people that for much of its time, the opposite of Conservatism had been liberalism, even suggesting that

> he [the liberal] differs much more from the collectivist radical of today than does the conservative ... One of the fundamental traits of the conservative attitude is a fear of change, a timid distrust of the new as such, while the liberal position is based on courage and confidence, on a preparedness to let change run its course even if we cannot predict where it will lead ... The conservatives ... lack the faith in the spontaneous forces of adjustment which makes the liberal accept changes without apprehension, even though he does not know how the necessary adaptations will be brought about. It is, indeed, part of the liberal attitude to assume that, especially in the economic field, the self-regulating forces of the market will somehow bring about the required adjustments to new conditions, although no one can foretell how they will do this in a particular instance.

Accepting 'changes without apprehension' is nowhere in the conservative tradition, and rightly so. Indeed, it could be argued that those affected most by such 'changes' are generally not those arguing for them.

Hayek expressed a belief that the free market would result in 'movement for movement's sake' and a relentless progress towards an unclear and ill-defined end point, letting 'change run its course even if we cannot predict where it will lead'. This might be a reasonable worldview, and it is certainly an articulate, fascinating and well-argued one, but it's pretty clear that it is not conservative.

After the 1980s, the word 'conservatism' was increasingly used to mean 'market liberalism' or even economic libertarianism. Its narrow definition of 'freedom', in some quarters, as being purely the freedom to make money was not one that previous generations of politicians would have recognised, and community institutions have all lost ground in recent decades as a result. There was no consideration of the loss of agency that comes from losing economic power, or the fact that this freedom can only be made complete in a social whole.

This transformation in the Tory Party was also accompanied by a considerable rewriting of its history – a belief that the return to laissez-faire was a return to a lost, but true, faith. As Ian Gilmour put it:

This Thatcherite triumphalism was reflected in the writings of a new generation of Thatcherite historians. These scholars produced a new reading of post-war history which, echoing the speeches of the new party leaders, closely resembled the existing left-wing analysis. They agreed with the socialist view that after years of compromise the Conservative Party was at last following its 'true' principles. Like their socialist counterparts, these observers added spice to their account by disparaging their party's former leaders. Every post-war Conservative Prime Minister, it emerged, had deviated from the true creed, although some were undoubtedly worse than others, and Winston Churchill needed to be handled with care.

This created a myth that the sole object of the Conservatives pre-1975 was 'managing decline'. Even if you put aside the stronger GDP growth, inflation, productivity and unemployment numbers in the 1950s, for example, this is not a thesis that stands up to the slightest scrutiny. When tariff reform and imperial preference were proposed by Joseph Chamberlain and, later, Stanley Baldwin, the ideas might have been criticised for being unworkable, but nobody in their right mind would describe them as being unambitious or 'managing decline'. Similarly, the policies of the 1951–64 Conservative government were deeply ambitious, with Harold Macmillan, among others, making clear that their goal was to reverse any relative decline and transform the way in which industry was run.

If the first element of the new ethos was restoring the market order, the second element was an attempt to restore national pride and some element of 'sovereignty'. Undoubtedly Thatcher's bravery and the Falklands victory marked a turning point for national morale, with a perception that the UK was no longer a country in decline. Her rhetoric during her time in office became increasingly attached to the concept of national sovereignty.

Nevertheless, the first, economic, element of the rebirth of economic liberalism was in direct contrast to the second. One of the conservative institutions that is inevitably weakened by an unfettered free market is undoubtedly the nation state. The actual and unintended consequences of neo-liberal reforms, which were then replicated in many other countries, were to speed up the pace of globalisation and reduce the ability of the British nation to act independently.

One of the first acts of the Thatcher government upon entering No. 10 in 1979 was to remove exchange controls. This undoubtedly had an important role to play in creating an environment for the revival of the City of London as the pre-eminent global financial centre, and the tight capital controls that existed in the late 1970s were almost worthy of a siege economy. The power of the change was such that nobody in politics, from the populist right to the hard left, would possibly argue for the return of capital controls today. This reform were symbolic, however, of a desire to rapidly increase the pace of globalisation and use the threat of capital flight to reduce the capacity for independent decision-making by a nation state. In such a case, the market was sovereign, and the actual power of the nation state was greatly diminished.

This is just one example of how one goal of revived laissez-faire subsumed the other. When national sovereignty and the desire to harness the dynamism of the market clashed, it was always going to be the market that won. Britain might have been a prouder nation by the end of the Thatcher period, her leadership during the time of Reagan and Gorbachev might have given us more of a punch on the global stage, but the actual power of the British state to pursue a genuinely independent policy had, in many ways, been weakened. As John Gray put it, 'The sovereign nation-state was glorified just at the historical moment when those who elevated it declared it to be economically redundant.'

The American political philosopher Michael Sandel also touched upon the impact of this renewal of laissez-faire when he argued that it led to 'devalued national identities and allegiances'.

As goods and capital and people flowed freely across national borders those who stood astride the global economy valorised cosmopolitan identities ... [they argued that] the real political divide ... was open versus closed ... this implied that critics ... were closed minded rather than open minded, tribal rather than global.

The attitude of economic liberals towards corporate takeovers best illuminates the difference between political patriotism and economic globalism. As Alex Brummer, now of the *Daily Mail* and formerly of *The Guardian*, has set out, successive governments have made British firms more prone to foreign takeovers than any other country in the Western world. This is an explicit impact of government policy and it has been since the 1980s. Most other countries have a much more intensive response to foreign takeovers, particularly of core assets.

This was illustrated by David Cameron, who, when pressed about the potential impact of Kraft's disgraceful takeover of a lean, well-run business like Cadburys, argued that the government shouldn't act because, 'we are an open global economy. We cannot start creating ownership barriers, trade barriers and other barriers.' This, of course, ignored the fact that almost every other country takes a more interventionist approach than the UK. UK firms are more prone to foreign takeover, which far outweighs the apparently associated benefit of giving UK firms the ability to acquire companies overseas. It also means that research and development tends to move to the home country of the owning firm, weakening the UK's manufacturing industry further. Thirty-nine per cent of patents in the UK are owned by foreign corporations. This compares to 11.8 per cent in the USA, 3.7 per cent in France and 13.7 per cent in the European Union as a whole. Once again, laissez-faire ramped up the rhetoric of the nation, but reduced its actual power.

This contrast between a desire for national self-determination and the internationalising impact of global markets is also illustrated by Mrs Thatcher's approach to the European Union. Her rhetoric was often strident about the EU and her most passionate modern-day adherents are particularly fond of quoting her late career speeches on the subject. The 'No, No, No' rejection of monetary union is one such example and another is the famous speech in Bruges in 1989. The latter is actually much more nuanced and complicated than many today give it credit for, and the same might be said of Thatcher's approach to Europe as a whole. Indeed, her ultimate rejection of the EU was, in many ways, a by-product of her attempt to use its institutions to impose Thatcherite reform on a continental scale, namely, to introduce the single market across the European Union and to remove all barriers to trade across the EU. In many ways, the modern European Union, with its strict single market rules and strictly orthodox fiscal guidelines, represents the attempted implementation of economic liberalism at a continental level (and in a way that tends to avoid democratic checks and balances). As Mrs Thatcher said in her Lancaster House speech in 1988:

> Just think for a moment what a prospect that is. A single market without barriers – visible or invisible – giving you direct and un-hindered access to the purchasing power of over 300 million of the world's wealthiest and most prosperous people … Britain has given the lead … We recognised that if Europe was going to be more than a slogan then we must get the basics right. That meant action

... Action to get rid of the barriers. Action to make it possible for insurance companies to do business throughout the Community. Action to let people practise their trades and professions freely throughout the Community. Action to remove the customs barriers and formalities so that goods can circulate freely and without time-consuming delays. Action to make sure that any company could sell its goods and services without let or hindrance. Action to secure free movement of capital throughout the Community.

A logical consequence of greater European integration through the single market and the introduction of a new raft of rules was to strengthen the European polity at the expense of national ones. As we've seen, this followed a more substantial period of removal of power from national government across a whole range of issues, from takeover policy to exchange and capital controls. The new dogma was that globalisation made nation states and the whim of national electorates futile against the might of the market. Nationalistic rhetoric became more a part of economic libertarianism with the realisation that the logical consequence of liberalising actions was to limit the power of the nation state at the hands of the market.

SOCIAL PEACE OR ECONOMIC EFFICIENCY? LAISSEZ-FAIRE AND ENGLAND'S FORGOTTEN TOWNS

It's still difficult to meet somebody who can consider the renewal of laissez-faire, personified in the UK by Thatcherism, in a dispassionate way. The wounds are still too raw; its physical impact on different parts of the country, from Consett or Barnsley to Canary Wharf, is still visible. Some Tories, often opposed to venerating leaders or hero worship, describe Margaret Thatcher as 'the saviour of the nation', while opponents still talk of her with ill-concealed hatred, seen to its most devastating artistic effect in Elvis Costello's 'Tramp the Dirt Down'.

Keith Joseph famously argued that the post-war UK had 'bought social peace at the expense of economic efficiency.' The earlier part of the Keynesian consensus was effective at delivering both, while the latter part emphatically delivered neither. A question that emerges from Joseph's dictum is whether the period of economic liberalism delivered economic efficiency, social peace or neither. If it delivered economic efficiency, was the price paid in social peace worth it? And was the short-term 'economic efficiency' genuinely delivered in post-industrial towns?

Despite the socially conservative instincts beneath Thatcherite rhetoric, its impact on society was in many ways deeply unconservative. There's little doubt that the Thatcher government caused bigger changes to society than any since that brought about between 1940 and 1950 by the wartime coalition and the Attlee governments. And this impact was possibly greater in those towns that suffered from deindustrialisation than anywhere else.

Social issues emerging from deindustrialisation, including levels of drug and alcohol addiction and high divorce rates, have had a particular impact on towns that once relied on heavy industry. As academics from Sheffield Hallam University have made clear, the long-term impact of the changes impacted by laissez-faire in the 1980s are still being felt today. They found that 'the highest claimant rates – 10 per cent or more of all 16–64-year-olds – are nearly all in older industrial areas', and that this shift of people out of the labour market has caused long-term pressure on the public finances. They also found that low pay in these areas depresses tax revenue and increases spending on in-work benefits: 'Spending on Tax Credits, for example, exceeds £850 a year per adult of working age in much of older industrial Britain – double the level in parts of southern England.'

A free market dogmatism also failed to address the real and substantial problems faced by towns that had lost their primary industry. It is now clear that merely 'rolling back the state' wasn't sufficient to allow a flowering of entrepreneurialism and growth in many areas. Pure laissez-faire would have expected companies to automatically relocate or for individuals to move to where the jobs and opportunities were. In this case, the dogma ignored both the desire of people to be close to their communities and their families and the importance of the state in providing both the infrastructure to attract business and the skills to allow people to prosper. Where Thatcherism did use the state to do this, whether it be in encouraging Nissan to Sunderland or finance to Canary Wharf, there were some genuine success stories, but they were part of a piecemeal approach that depended too much on the market and too little on the state.

As Sandel identified, the identification of economic success with merit created a hubris among those who succeeded (often actually due to family connections) and feelings of anger among those 'left behind'. He argued that, for those left behind by three decades of market-driven globalisation, the problem is not only wage stagnation and the loss of jobs; it is also the loss of social esteem. It is not only about unfairness; it is also about humiliation ... Conducting our public discourse as if it were possible to outsource moral judgement to markets, or to procedures of liberal public reason has created a narrow, impoverished public discourse, a vacuum of public meaning ... Three decades of market-driven globalisation have hollowed out democratic public discourse, disempowered ordinary citizens and prompted a populist backlash that seeks to cloth the public square with an intolerant, vengeful nationalism.

Beneath the sheen, structural issues remained in the British economy, with a simplistic belief in the value of the market on one side and the value of the state on the other obscuring questions over how to overcome these issues. The dominant concept of the revived laissez-faire, whether expressed through Blair's market that was 'indifferent to tradition' or Thatcher's idea that 'you can't buck the market', was that individuals and communities were effectively powerless against the all-powerful market. In both cases, communities had to *adapt* to these powerful forces, and it was beyond their means to change them. It was this that led many communities to feel a loss of agency and to go on to express a desire to 'take back control'.

At the same time, however, the decades from 1979 have seen many people become better off and able to live the lives that they choose with reduced fear of bigotry or discrimination. It's impossible to judge the past few decades in a linear way. The advance of social

freedom in recent decades is undoubtedly a positive, but it resulted in a progressivism that had divorced itself from economics and
stopped considering economic alternatives. Economic liberalisation
was certainly necessary to turn around a country that was facing
economic stagnation. The fact that this hardened into a dogma and
seemed to cause a hollowing out of much of the conservative political tradition risked consistently looking back to the solutions of the
late 1970s to answer the very different questions of today.

Thatcherism made Britain a more entrepreneurial society, but
also a less united one. It made people trust institutions less, trust
government less and be more concerned with individual advancement at the expense of community bonds. Some people and some
places benefited massively from the Thatcher revolution, but
others were devastated, often losing their sense of individual or
collective worth. The Thatcher legacy was neither wholly negative
nor wholly positive, but there is no doubt its consequences are
still being felt today.

THE RELEVANCE OF ECONOMIC LIBERALISM TO TODAY'S ISSUES

Through her power of personality, which continued right until
her death, Mrs Thatcher achieved a devoted following within the
Tory Party that hadn't been achieved by any previous leader. She
imprinted a clear ideological stamp on the party that meant most
who followed her in the decades that followed were devotees of
her form of laissez-faire (albeit a less pluralist, more caricatured
form than she herself carried out in office; the electoral disasters

of 2001 and 2005 were based on manifestos that were much more 'Thatcherite' than Mrs Thatcher). The circumstances of her ejection from Downing Street meant that wounds opened within the Tory Party that have never really closed, and that betrayal narrative, previously common on the centre-left but not the centre-right, became an utterly toxic one.

The power of her ideas and the urgency of the situation she faced at the time remain remarkable. Although we now know that these ideas have also had damaging side effects, it's impossible not to still respect the sheer human impact and determination of one person. But that doesn't mean that conservatism should become utopian or see its ideas frozen in time. The problems and issues have changed and there is little that a static ideology can do to address them. Too much of modern economic liberalism seems one-eyed, unaware that today's problems need nuance rather than dogma, and seemingly uncaring of the losers from economic change.

Homilies to economic freedom meant a lot when tax rates were at over 90 per cent and you had to wait three weeks for a choice of two telephones. Economic freedom means less, however, when people have seen their lives blighted by economic insecurity and stagnant wages. The ability to have a meal delivered or order a relatively inexpensive taxi from your mobile phone does not make up for the lack of a secure job or the inability to even contemplate getting on the housing ladder.

An important question is whether Thatcherism is a viable philosophy for governance today or whether it was simply a response to specific societal issues and economic pressures that arose in the mid- to late 1970s. As Skidelsky wrote:

Thatcherism may have been necessary to break out of the corporatist and bureaucratic impasse of the late 1970s; but the analysis was oversimple, the means crude and mean. More fundamentally, Thatcherism as an economic and social philosophy – as a basis for the long-term government of Britain – is seriously one sided. In this respect it resembles the Manchester Liberalism of the early nineteenth century which energised the economy but had to be tamed, moralised and intellectually refined before it was fit to establish a new social order.

It remains important that the economic dynamism that economic liberals rightly say the market produces is encouraged and maintained. That is, however, only half the story. This alone can't help to repair the economic and social fabric in those areas that suffered from industrial decline. Nor can it provide the infrastructure necessary to ensure that these areas prosper in the future. A more nuanced approach compared to the simplistic and dogmatic approach of pure economic liberalism is necessary in order to ensure that prosperity is spread more widely and society becomes less fractured. As I'll make clear, an older tradition of One Nation, which was largely lost in the rush to economic liberalism, provides this nuance and should be embraced.

CHAPTER SIX

THE LIMITS OF IDENTITY? IDENTITY LIBERALISM AND THE DIMINUTION OF SOLIDARITY

England is perhaps the only great country whose intellectuals
are ashamed of their own nationality. In left-wing circles it is
always felt that there is something slightly disgraceful in being
an Englishman and that it is a duty to snigger at every English
institution, from horse racing to suet puddings. It is a strange fact,
but it is unquestionably true that almost any English intellectual
would feel more ashamed of standing to attention during
'God save the King' than of stealing from a poor box.
– George Orwell, 'The Lion and the Unicorn'

Economic liberalism, as we have seen, has helped to create atomisation, while also tackling many of the economic problems that seemed chronic in the late 1970s. At much the same time, a form of identity liberalism also gained momentum. Like economic liberalism, it arose to deal with some important problems, when discrimination was common and steps had to be taken to ensure that the country became more tolerant and a better place to live for women, gay people and ethnic minorities. Real progress has been made and British society is a less prejudiced place than it was several decades ago. For example, in 1987, three-quarters of people felt that homosexuality was 'always or mostly wrong'. That figure is now less than a quarter.

We know, however, that more still needs to be done. It's still essential that this progress is maintained and that prejudice is eliminated. Unemployment is much higher among young black men than young white men. The disparity between male and female pay remains too high. Violence against LGBT people remains a real threat.

To many of its greatest devotees, however, identity liberalism has moved beyond tackling specific problems and has become a hardened and dogmatic ideology. As a consequence, 'identity' trumps other factors such as nationality and local community. What started as something that aimed to tackle known issues now risks becoming divisive, as the 'I' of identity overtakes the 'we'. At its worst, identity liberalism has become a caricature, removing agency from people and saying that they should be defined purely by their race, gender or sexuality, with uniform (generally left-wing) political views. A recent example was the level of liberal handwringing that accompanied Boris Johnson appointing the most diverse Cabinet in history. Labour frontbencher Clive Lewis was moved to suggest that Conservative Party chairman James Cleverly and other non-white Cabinet members 'had to sell their soul and self-respect to get there', while editor of the hard-left Canary, Kerry-Anne Mendoza, decided that 'someone from a minority group who chooses to serve in a far-right government is no longer a person of colour'. Such hysterical, self-evidently absurd statements show that, in many ways, identity politics has eaten itself and gives people no ability to decide their own opinions beyond their 'group'. This is patently divisive and wrong.

The most extreme practitioners of identity liberalism have *actively* sought to diminish elements of communal and national identity, particularly British history and iconography. This has served to put them at odds with many people in the post-industrial towns we have been discussing, who still hold a strong sense of patriotism and pride in their country's history. Another element of identity liberalism has deepened this void: an emphasis on 'out' or 'victim groups' has meant that white working-class men in particular have tended to be ignored or deprioritised. This has had an obvious impact on England's forgotten towns and their inhabitants.

THE DENUNCIATION OF PATRIOTISM AND THE RISE OF IDENTITY POLITICS

Two events in 2018 had the rare effect of unifying much of England. Both the wedding of the Duke and Duchess of Sussex and England's electrifying run to the World Cup semi-final had the nation gripped and saw record TV audiences.

There were, of course, dissenting voices, and many of these voices were heard among the liberal intellectuals so memorably deplored by Orwell. *The Guardian* was full of opinion pieces denouncing people for having an interest in the royal wedding. Emma Dent Coad MP, Member for Kensington, was symbolic of this when she announced that she had 'no interest in the royal wedding and ... won't be shamed into silence'. Her lack of interest only extended to a lengthy article in a national newspaper and numerous tweets.

Similarly, dissenting voices were heard as England advanced on its most successful World Cup campaign for almost three decades. *The Guardian* was peppered with columns about why certain columnists wouldn't be supporting England. Various 'woke' Twitter accounts anxiously imposed a flag of England's upcoming rivals on their Twitter profile page. The police warned football fans before the World Cup not to fly the St George's Cross, on the basis that it was, apparently, 'imperialistic', and 'can cause antagonism'. In an absurd move, rightly ignored by its workers, the Royal Mail banned postmen from flying England flags during the tournament.

The England World Cup campaign was also accompanied by various commentators musing that the sporting event should mark the beginning of 'reclaiming the England flag'. Similar comments were made about the Union Flag during the London Olympics. In all cases, they are absurd. The only people who think that our national flag has been 'captured' by the far right are generally those who denigrate patriotism and look to diminish British history. Only 14 per cent of English people regard the Union Flag as a racist symbol and less than a quarter think the same of the St George's Cross. Yet many on the left continue to sneer at the flag and its supporters, notably Emily Thornberry, now shadow Foreign Secretary, when she sent her infamous 'image from #Rochester' via Twitter.

Almost every sense of shared history or national belonging is denigrated by these national self-flagellators. There is a near-frantic urge among them to find past quotations by national heroes that would have been less acceptable in today's climate. Afua Hirsch made a ludicrous call in 2017 for Nelson to be removed from Trafalgar Square. Hirsch gained the 'woke' credibility she was looking for and almost 40,000 people shared her preposterous article. Similarly, an unknown professor at Birmingham City University was happy to denounce Winston Churchill as an 'imperialist racist', arguing that the 'history of this country is built on racism'. This controversy then gathered new life when an obscure Green member of the Scottish Parliament used similar arguments to denounce Churchill. Shadow Chancellor John McDonnell then described the great wartime leader as a 'villain'.

This attention-grabbing approach was also adopted by Aaron Bastani, advocate of 'automated luxury communism'. Shortly before the hundredth anniversary of the Armistice and doubtless aware of the potential for column inches that his remarks would draw, Bastani decided to denounce the poppy appeal and the Royal British Legion. He ludicrously commented that 'the poppy appeal is grotesque, it has a kind of triumphalist militarism to it. It's racist, right, it's white supremacist.'

Based on these arguments, Britain's history is almost uniquely one of shame. The Empire is regarded as an unadulterated sin and even the saving of Europe from Nazi tyranny is now denounced as an outdated nostalgia. Labour leader Jeremy Corbyn has called on the 'injustices' of British history to be taught in schools. He seems to share the view of many in the left-wing establishment that such 'injustices' formed a dominant part of our national story.

That such a view is not felt by the bulk of the population should come as little surprise. A recent YouGov poll found that 9 per cent of 18–24-year-olds and 3 per cent of over 65s said that they were 'embarrassed' to be English. There is a real suspicion that this proportion would be considerably higher among the political and media class.

THE DECONSTRUCTION OF NATIONAL MYTHS

The beliefs of much of the modern left (and much of the modern right) towards their country is oddly reminiscent of George Canning's famous quote about the Jacobin: 'A steady patriot of the world alone, The friend of every country but his own.'

When unifying symbols are deconstructed, so is our sense of unity as a nation.

It's right to suggest that this is hardly a new phenomenon. Already in this chapter, I have quoted from the 1790s and the 1940s. What is new about the modern national self-flagellation is that it has become entrenched as an orthodoxy in many powerful circles.

Whereas previously such views might well have stayed within the student union or the crankish fringe, they are now held, almost as a matter of course, in large swathes of academia, politics and the media. This is illustrated starkly by David Goodhart in his excellent *Road to Somewhere*, where he made the distinction between two groups – Anywheres and Somewheres. 'Somewheres', by his definition, are rooted in place, are patriotic and less likely to be university educated. They also represent around three quarters of the population. The 'anywheres' are urban, very socially liberal and have little time for what they see as the anachronism of patriotism. While representing a quarter or less of the population, they represent well over 90 per cent of the elite. Their views, despite not being shared by most people in the country, therefore dominate the nation's political, academic and elite conversation – leaving others feeling embittered that their views are seen as somehow illegitimate.

This was also picked up by former Labour Cabinet minister John Denham, who attacked the 'marginalisation' of English identity by 'elite liberal Britain'. According to Denham, 'this anti-English fraction is over-represented within the institutions of government, within the leadership of the public sector, within corporate capitalism and in academia (in short, a large part of what is sometimes called the elite). It is, of course, found within politics, and on the left in particular.'

Complaints about a 'liberal metropolitan elite' are often wearing and misguided, but in cases where patriotism is maligned and shared history and collective memory is weakened, the elite in many parts of life have had their own role to play in driving distrust, division and disengagement.

As many commentators have pointed out, the intellectual impetus behind a desire to diminish the bonds of national identity lies in a mix of postmodernism and identity politics. Postmodernism can be a nebulous and over-used term, but it's critique about metanarratives, particularly around issues such as national identity and religion, provides an important clue as to why we are where we are today.

Similarly, terms like 'identity politics' don't deserve to be disparaged unthinkingly. As mentioned earlier, LGBT people, women and ethnic minorities have a much greater ability to live a fruitful life, devoid of prejudice, than was the case in the past, but great challenges are still felt by all these groups. The rise of identity liberalism has, however, diminished solidarity and the social contract through the desire of some to see politics and citizenship purely through this 'identity' lens.

In this landscape, the most important identifying factors tend to be gender, ethnicity, sexuality and religion, with the world often divided between 'the oppressors' and 'the oppressed'.

Such a point of view is based on a distorted and distorting view of power structures, society and history. It argues that power has always been abused and that the unifying politics of nation, or even class, is deceptive. It removes human agency, relegates certain groups to permanent victim or oppressed status and positions others in the permanent role of oppressor. It is also a recipe for permanent division.

By reducing straight white men, in particular, to permanent oppressor status, it also indulges in crude reductionism. The British trade union movement, for example, was predominantly established to serve the interests of straight white men, and few would argue that the straight white men who served in the trenches of the First World War or the miners who died of black lung had somehow been oppressors or were at the top of a power structure.

This lens of oppressor and oppressed dominates the thinking

of post-modern liberals. So-called oppressor groups are always to be condemned and the oppressed are to be sided with. Hence, much of the modern left makes clear its discomfiture with much of Western history and regards it as its business to always side with the group it regards as oppressed. This typology tends to lead to a dichotomy of 'the West = bad, others = good', and, put more severely, 'Israel = bad, others = good'. This absurd logic has led some to march for human rights on a Saturday and side with butchery in Iran or Syria on a Sunday.

IDENTITY LIBERALISM AND ENGLAND'S FORGOTTEN TOWNS

While identity is the primary concern of the ruling elite, it's unlikely that the white working class and, in particular, white working-class men will be prioritised. This has been particularly damaging to those living in England's forgotten towns, as some of the most profound and important issues are faced by white, working-class men, and the instinct of much of identity liberalism is to ignore or diminish these concerns.

White, working-class boys, for example, have the worst results at school other than Romani children. This comparative difference in performance isn't just at GCSE level, but is reflected across educational performance from the age of five. Official Department for Education statistics show that white working-class boys are less likely than other groups to be sufficiently literate or numerate by the age of five. White British boys are also less likely than any other group to attend higher education.

Shadow Education Secretary Angela Rayner has argued that an emphasis on race and gender equality has had a 'negative impact on the food chain for white working boys'. As she rightly points out, the initial focus on race and gender was based on problems and discrimination that did actually exist and needed to be addressed. This has meant that issues around the attainment of white working-class boys was originally forgotten, before being ignored. Only now is it being regarded as an issue that needs to be addressed.

The emphasis on identity politics has also contributed to, and in many cases worsened, the crisis of masculinity being felt in many post-industrial towns. Whereas work, in a steelwork or mine for example, used to provide a sense of meaning to many, the shift to other types and models of work, which are generally more insecure, has also produced a reduction in self-worth. This has been combined with rapid economic and social changes and, in many cases, substantial alterations to the demographic makeup of a town or village. Hence, the modern landscape has become one of economic and cultural uncertainty, where modern snobbery against the white working class has come to be regarded as almost legitimate.

Research by Gidron and Hall, academics from Princeton and Harvard, has identified the perceived decline in social standing felt by white working-class men, describing this as 'status anxiety rooted in broader processes of social marginalisation'. They argue that there are

good reasons for thinking that economic and cultural developments have combined to depress the subjective social status of

white working-class men ... Since social status is typically con-
ferred by levels of income and the quality of one's occupation,
shifting patterns of employment that have eliminated well-paid,
medium-skill jobs and forced many men into more precarious positions may well have undercut their own sense of where they stand
in society. At the same time, shifts in cultural frameworks, marked
by an increasing emphasis in mainstream discourse on racial and
gender equality, may have threatened ... subjective social status.

An emphasis on identity politics is also to ignore the point that
viewing politics primarily through the lens of gender, sexuality or
otherwise is not the way in which most people view their identity. Such a push towards identity politics has been overly abstract
and has ignored how people view themselves and react to other
members of their community. The fact that many people in working-class communities chose Brexit was almost as much of a shock
to the modern left as when the proletariat chose country over
class in 1914. And they both arose for the same reason: because
the people's alleged spokesmen and women failed to understand
that the primary loyalty of most people today continues to be the
nation state, especially when a nation is unified by language and
history. The caricaturing of Brexit as a piece of white, English,
imperial nostalgia from angry white men is not only nonsensical
and flawed, it ignores the fact that a third of BME voters, 49 per
cent of women, 40 per cent of 25–34-year-olds and almost 53 per
cent of voters in Wales voted to leave.

A shift towards economic and identity liberalism has brought
many benefits, but by emphasising the individual over the collective

it has also led to reduced community cohesion, increasing loneliness and isolation. As the likes of Robert Putnam, David Brooks, Charles Murray, Yuval Levin, George Packer and others have recognised in the USA, modern social, cultural, economic and political life is less cohesive and more fragmented. Economic cohesion has been damaged by the rising share of wealth going to the very rich while the incomes of others stagnated, political cohesion has been damaged by increasing party polarisation, demographic cohesion has been impacted by rising immigration and attachments to large institutions have been replaced by flexible networks. As Brooks and Levin argue, a hollowing out of the middle has resulted in 'bifurcated concentration', with an emphasis on communal acts or 'being part of the congregation' replaced by mere identity.

What these American thinkers have picked up is very much a feature of life in the UK. Economic and identity liberalism has produced a society that feels more divided, more bifurcated than ever and has reduced bonds of cohesion and a feeling of 'we' as a country or a community. This economic and identity liberalism has gained almost consensus approval among many politicians, as well as figures in the media and business. Neither form of liberalism has, though, gained widespread approval among the bulk of the people.

THE POSITIVE NATURE OF NATIONAL IDENTITY

Whereas identity politics is divisive, a focus on national identity, for all of its weaknesses, can be both unifying and positive. It also represents the instinctive patriotism that is still strongly felt in the post-industrial towns that have been the focus of this book.

Consider again the shared moments that emerged from recent years – royal weddings, World Cup runs, the London Olympics. They all brought the country together through a shared sense of purpose. Collective memories, shared identity and so-called meta narratives – whether it be saving the world from fascism by standing alone, or being the birthplace of parliamentary democracy and the rule of law – are things that hold us together.

Orwell's assertion in 1940 that 'there is something distinctive and recognizable in English civilization' is still as clear today and, as he suggested, this 'is continuous, it stretches into the future and the past, there is something in it that persists, as in a living creature'. Despite the attempts of many on the left, we remain a distinct nation, with shared touchpoints and collective memories. Despite efforts to focus on less transcendent identities, this unified form of identity remains strong. To paraphrase Orwell, there is still something distinctly different about England; we are much more than a collection of 60 million individuals.

Orwell came close to the perfect analogy, with his description of England as a slightly disjointed family, but a family all the same: 'Still, it is a family. It has its private language and its common memories, and at the approach of an enemy it closes its ranks. A family with the wrong members in control – that, perhaps, is as near as one can come to describing England in a phrase.'

As we have seen, despite the efforts of intellectuals and others, pride in the country and its achievements remains strong among most of the population. It was hard to turn a corner of England during the World Cup run and not see a St George's Cross hanging somewhere. Goals saw total strangers embracing each other, united by their joint nationhood and shared reference points. The royal wedding saw similar scenes of unity – much mocked but clear and often spontaneous.

There's also little evidence that English or British patriotism is as exclusive as some liberals would believe. Those who think that Englishness is somehow 'exclusive' should reflect on the fact that only 12 per cent of BME voters don't agree that St George's Day should be a bank holiday, and 54 per cent of voters believe that paying more attention to Englishness would unite communities.

English identity, of course, has more to it than suet puddings, pillar boxes or even tea. There's so much that we have to be proud of – so many elements of this shared identity that we have to celebrate. Fundamental to this is the concept of the 'freeborn Englishman' – an idea popularised by the Levellers, with its roots in the Magna Carta. It's a romantic but important conception that Englishness is rooted in freedom and liberty, something ingrained in the soil and the people, given voice by Levellers, Chartists, suffragettes.

These liberties are expressed through Parliament and institutions. Michael Foot argued that 'no comparable institution ... has shaped so continuously the life and society of any Western European state.' John Lilburne, the great Leveller, talked of 'the free Commons of England – the real and essential body politic'.

The English language, from Shakespeare and the Authorised Version through to Byron and Blake, is also a source of enormous pride. Eighty-nine per cent of English people told YouGov that they felt proud of the English language, and think it plays an important part in their sense of Englishness. This uniquely English use of language is still very clear in the lyrics of people like Alex Turner and Ray Davies, as it is English music, architecture and culture that have spread English identity globally. More locally, it is embodied in the English pub, English humour, the unique beauty of the English countryside, the great games of football and cricket that England has given the world (the global success story of the Premier League is an example).

These factors – the English language, the all-embracing popularity of English sport and culture, the continuing strength of the economy, the respect in which the military is held – all add up to bolstering our international reputation and providing potential unifying factors for a divided nation. This isn't to return to the banality of 'Cool Britannia'; more to reflect the instinctive patriotism already felt by the bulk of the nation.

As we look to rebuild the UK and remould the social contract, we need to look beyond the twin philosophies – laissez-faire and identity politics – that have made society atomised by emphasising the individual over the collective. These common bonds and shared values could mark the foundation for a renewed national unity. The contrast with a fetish for identity politics couldn't be greater. Where a patriotism unites, a devotion to identity politics divides. The latter therefore cannot be the basis for a renewed social contract that brings the country together after a particularly divisive decade. For this reason, it should be rejected as an organising principle for society.

CHAPTER SEVEN

HOW LABOUR STOPPED STANDING FOR THE WORKERS

One thing that most of England's forgotten post-industrial towns had in common was that they generally returned Labour MPs. The party had been formed to stand up for the interests of workers in these towns and even after the closure of the industries on which they depended, still regarded the Labour Party as the natural guardian of their interests.

In some of these towns, voters almost saw the Labour Party as a part of their extended family. As Marquand put it in *The Progressive Dilemma*, in some close-knit mining communities, being Labour was an extension of being part of a working-class community.

In recent decades, that has fundamentally changed. Tony Blair's New Labour and then Jeremy Corbyn's hard-left Labour have transformed Labour from a working-class party of the towns to a middle-class party for professionals in cities. This has played another role in the political and economic marginalisation of voters in England's towns and has left many voters politically homeless.

As I'll set out in the concluding chapters, Labour's abandonment of their core support provides an opportunity for a party prepared to set out a bold and transformative project. Before that, however, it is worth considering how Labour shifted so dramatically from the party of workers to the party of urban hipsters.

WHAT WOULD CLEMENT DO?

I remember around the time of the Labour Party conferences that saw Jeremy Corbyn's rise to the leadership, there were dozens of these red T-shirts emblazoned with the face of the party's great wartime and post-war leader alongside the words 'What Would Clement Do?' The subtext was pretty obvious – that Clem would back Jeremy. The reality is, of course, much murkier.

As John Bew has set out in his excellent *Citizen Clem*, Attlee cannot be understood without reference to his great patriotism and love of country. This was, after all, a man who defied the rules in order to sign up to serve in the First World War. His was a belief that patriotism brought with it a sense of citizenship and a need to do right by your fellow man. This 'commonweal' was partially formed through a sense of mutual obligation that came through patriotism.

In a 1949 pamphlet entitled 'Labour Believes in Britain', the Attlee government talked about approaching the task of reform through

the British spirit – the effort to find practical solutions to practical

problems, but no less to aim at a high and comprehensive purpose
... [the aim of which is] to usher in the finest age in our history
– a buoyant age of adventure, progress and initiative, of unity in
common purpose and justified pride in our nation's greatness.

It's hard to imagine today's Labour Party, which seems run
through with national self-flagellation, using such language of
national pride and national potential.

Attlee's speech to the 1951 Labour Party conference helped illu-
minate his patriotic approach to socialism:

The crucial question of this election, on which every elector must
make up his or her mind, is this: What kind of society do you
want? We know the kind of society we want. We want a society
of free men and women – free from poverty, free from fear, able
to develop to the full their faculties in co-operation with their fel-
lows, everyone giving and having the opportunity to give service
to the community, everyone regarding his own private interest in
the light of the interest of others, and of the community; a society
bound together by rights and obligations, rights bringing obligations, obligations fulfilled bringing rights; a society free from gross
inequalities and yet not regimented nor uniform.

As Bew argues, 'the overlapping notions of citizenship, patriotism
and ethical socialism had been absolutely integral to Attlee's belief
system from the earliest years'. This notion wasn't restricted to the
Prime Minister of the great post-war reforming government. It
was something felt by ministers on both the left and right of the

Cabinet. Ernest Bevin, almost certainly the greatest Foreign Secretary of the twentieth century and a genuine lion of the Labour movement, had an unstinting patriotism and belief in the British people. This often brought him into conflict with the hard left, particularly over the establishment of NATO and the independent nuclear deterrent, on which Bevin famously declared:

> I don't want any other Foreign Secretary of this country to be talked to or at by a Secretary of State in the United States as I have just had in my discussions with Mr Byrnes. We've got to have this thing over here whatever it costs … We've got to have the bloody Union Jack on top of it.

Brian Brivati, in his excellent biography of Gaitskell, points out that most senior Labour politicians of this generation shared the innate patriotism of Attlee and Bevin. According to Brivati:

> Overlaying his personal struggles and his political obsession with power was his deep patriotism … His most characteristic political position was his attitude towards the Common Market: control over his country's destiny … He was, like all the leading Labour politicians of his generation, a patriot and a nationalist, who was sure that Britain had a genuine global role to play.

The 1945 Labour government was a substantial patriotic effort, formed on the basis that all members of the national community deserve a chance to play a part in that community.

An important element of this was its reflection of the strongly held patriotism of the working-class communities the party was established to represent. This patriotism was felt by working-class representatives, such as Bevin, but also by members of other classes, such as Gaitskell and Attlee. Hugh Dalton famously told G. D. H. Cole that Labour would only win power with 'the votes of the football crowds'. At this, Cole 'shuddered and turned away'.

Martin Pugh has described the concept of 'Tory Socialism', a combination of far-reaching domestic reform and belief in country and its institutions, whereby 'Tories and socialists often found themselves sharing common assumptions ... in opposition to the Liberal-Radical tradition'. As Pugh explains:

> The tradition had a vital electoral dimension in that Labour's patchy advance in some regions and localities is explicable in terms of its capacity to accommodate itself to the prevailing populist Toryism in working-class communities ... it proved remarkably durable and vigorous right through to the end of the twentieth century ... during both the First and Second World Wars the national crisis fostered working class patriotism and the common ground between Labour and Toryism.

This Tory socialism has all but disappeared as the Labour Party has become increasingly dominated by liberals and middle-class city dwellers. The bullying of the handful of Labour MPs who supported Leave in the 2016 referendum stands as evidence to that.

The crucial role that Attlee, Bevin, Morrison and Cripps played in the wartime coalition was essential to the defeat of the Nazis and also essential to Labour winning an overwhelming majority in 1945. Bevin's role was absolutely central in making sure that all of the resources of the country were mobilised and the closeness of the partnership was such that Attlee insisted on being a pall bearer at Churchill's funeral, describing the great wartime leader as 'an old opponent and a colleague, but always a friend ... the greatest Englishman of our time – I think the greatest citizen of the world of our time'.

The importance of Labour's working-class roots is essential to understanding this 'Tory Socialism', but it's also crucial when trying to discover what the party was and what it has lost. It's become a cliché to roll out the Harold Wilson quote that the Labour Party 'owes more to Methodism than Marx', but that doesn't make it any less true. The Labour Party was, of course, established through the Labour Representation Committee with the goal to have 'a distinct Labour group in Parliament, who shall have their own whips, and agree upon their policy, which must embrace a readiness to cooperate with any party which for the time being may be engaged in promoting legislation in the direct interests of labour'. In other words, to ensure that the interests of the working class were represented in Parliament, and to ensure that, in some cases, these interests were represented by working-class people. Needless to say, trade unions were absolutely essential to this, but so too were the Methodist churches, the friendly societies and other institutions of working-class life. In this way, the party was able to represent the institutions and traditions of working-class life.

Michael Foot, not himself from a working-class background, spoke of this when first becoming the MP for Ebbw Vale:

The people of industrial Wales are proud of their working-class tradition, proud of their working-class achievements and still as proud as ever of being working-class ... Men and women still believe that it is better to live in a real community than to set before themselves the idea of rising out of their class, spurning their great ancestry and kicking away the ladder.

This might have been romanticisation, but it encapsulated neatly how Labour saw their historic role of representing working-class communities. This also meant that many working-class communities, particularly in the north-east, Scotland and South Wales, came to regard Labour as part of their community and voted accordingly.

In many cases, the working-class representation reinforced a traditional-minded conservatism within Labour. The area around Consett is illustrative of this. Although certain local pit villages, such as Chopwell (nicknamed Little Moscow), had a radical left tradition, most of the Consett area was 'labourist', which Ralph Miliband described as 'an ideology of social reform, within the framework of capitalism, with no serious ambition of transcending that framework'. As such, the labourist tradition in the Consett area was relatively conservative; it had the goal of improving pay and conditions for workers, but also strongly represented the traditional views of working people. The town's historian argues that the 'Labour Party in the area was moderate and few places were more moderate than Consett or Stanley'. This was the tradition that was carried by people like Ernie Bevin, Jim Callaghan (with his famous homage to the language of Chaucer, Shakespeare and

Milton in opposing Common Market membership, one of many factors that led *The Economist* to label him 'Labour's Conservative') and Denis Healey – patriotic, strong on defence, resolutely anti-Marxist, but equally resolutely in favour of improving and extending workers' rights.

That tradition has all but died. As *The Economist* argued, 'Labour is no longer the party of the traditional working class.' In so many ways, Labour has, despite claims to the contrary, distanced itself from its traditional working-class base. It is more and more a middle-class party, with liberal views and, as we have seen, a focus on identity politics, both of which are detached from those working-class voters the party was set up to represent. The tragedy is that this has come at a time when the traditional working class has needed a voice more than ever. As the previous chapter has shown, white, working-class boys are the poorest performers in school (which doesn't stop prominent Labour activists talking of white privilege), while former industrial areas are in desperate need of economic and social renewal.

BLAIR AND THE WORKING CLASS: NOWHERE ELSE TO GO?

Blair's Labour did, in part, stay true to this old tradition. His experience in Sedgefield helped to inform many of the views he took on issues such as welfare and crime. Despite this, Labour became much more middle-class under his leadership. People from genuinely working-class backgrounds were little represented in his governments or in the party organisation. Instead, the party's voters became more middle class. In 1997, Blair gained an impressive 50 per cent of the skilled working-class vote and 59 per cent of the unskilled working-class vote with his communitarian message. By 2010, Labour's vote among the skilled working class had tumbled to 29 per cent and the unskilled working-class vote fell equally dramatically to 40 per cent.

The impact that Tony Blair made on British politics was profound and immediate. His polling adviser, Philip Gould, advised him that his first speech to the Labour Party conference should be 'so bold, so clear, so uncompromising that [it] confounds the electorate, forcing them to change their minds'.

Much of Blair's early rhetoric indicated that he understood the void that a combination of market liberalism and social individualism had created and the impact they had on communal institutions. Early Blair talked about the influence of Christian Socialists, such as John Macmurray, and the importance of societal bonds. According to Gould, for Macmurray:

> Hegel's notion of civil society, combined with Plato's belief in the ethical nature of citizenship, helped produce a new philosophy which rejected the laissez-faire stance of Adam Smith and the individualism of the Unitarians. In its place stood the concept of community through which the individual could realise himself.

Blair's government did show some determination to move on from a myopic obsession with pure market solutions. The minimum wage was introduced against the teeth of foolish Conservative opposition and vigorous warnings from the think tanks and commentators of the economically liberal right that it would cost millions of jobs. In reality, it was one of the most successful policies of the entire post-war period, having little, if any, impact on jobs, while at the same time improving productivity and, crucially, bringing about a substantial increase in the quality of life of some of the poorest people in society.

Such a shift away from pure laissez-faire was a welcome one, as was the redistributive momentum behind the introduction of tax credits, but New Labour, despite its early communitarian leanings, didn't really challenge the economic settlement. If anything, later Blair was more besotted with the dynamic impact of the free market than Mrs Thatcher herself. As Sandel argues, Blair and other 'Third Way' leaders, such as Schroder and Clinton,

moderated but consolidated the market faith. They softened the harsh edges of unfettered markets, but did not challenge the central premise that market mechanisms are the primary instruments for achieving the public good. In line with this faith, they embraced a market-driven version of globalisation and welcomed the growing financialisation of the economy.

Government played a role in regenerating major northern and Midlands cities, with the hugely renewed urban centres in places like Newcastle, Manchester and Liverpool owing much to the vision of the Blair governments. But much of this regeneration was skin deep; many of the towns and villages that surrounded the regenerated centres continued their cycle of economic and social decline. Well-meaning schemes, such as Pathfinder programmes, weren't sufficient to deliver more dynamic economies or social progress. Government centralised into a stack of national, unelected agencies, which the Thatcher government developed and Major and Blair expanded massively. The story of the 1980s onwards was of an empowered centre, an empowered market and increasingly atomised communities.

If Blair shared Thatcher's love for the dynamism of markets, he also shared her passion for the financial services sector. While manufacturing as a proportion of the economy fell from 17 per cent to 10 per cent between 1997 and 2010, financial services played a bigger and bigger role. Both Blair and Gordon Brown were happy to boast about their 'light touch' regulation of the city, both seeing it as a way of creating the wealth that could then be redistributed. As we have seen, however, this left the British economy dangerously unbalanced both regionally and sectorally, which was to scar the country for over a decade when the crash arrived in 2008. New Labour failed to challenge the predominance of financial services or even to begin to develop an economic model that could achieve a balance between economic dynamism and social justice, or to ensure that the benefits of economic growth were felt more widely. Instead, globalisation and support for European integration became substitutes for an active economic policy.

For later Blair, outside of fiscal policy, there was no role for the state in the economy. Equally, it was only when recession hit that New Labour seriously turned their mind towards industrial strategy, meaning that over a decade that could have been focused on creating a more balanced economic model was effectively wasted.

Blairism shifted from being a communitarian doctrine to a fundamentally liberal one, which emphasised the duo of economic and identity liberalism just when the side effects of both were becoming clear. It was sufficiently in hock to the free movement of capital to regard the continued flourishing of the City of London as one of its great achievements (at least until the bubble burst in 2008). Blair was increasingly intoxicated by the market and the belief that globalisation (created by states and potentially controlled by states) was a force of nature, which couldn't be disputed or altered.

His 2005 speech to the Labour Party conference could have been written by one of the free market think tanks that populate Westminster and Washington, DC. As David Goodhart has commented, it would come as a surprise to many that the man who gave that speech represented the party that had been established to protect people from the impacts of economic change. In the speech, he said that debating globalisation was the same as debating 'whether autumn should follow summer'. Blair put forward a political philosophy that was, in his own words, 'indifferent to tradition ... unforgiving of frailty ... no respecter of past reputations ... [with] no custom or practice'.

Indifferent to tradition ... No respecter of past reputations. This was the result of an apparently 'conservative' worldview introduced in the 1970s. It was a conservatism that had forgotten how to conserve.

No forgiver of frailty. These were words uttered by the leader of a party that was still, apparently, a 'democratically socialist' one. Is it any wonder that the damn burst so utterly in 2016?

Thatcher may have removed many of the economic powers of national governments, but it was Blair who did more than any other Prime Minister to diminish the power of the nation state against the so-called might of the global marketplace. Despite this, globalisation of the kind described by Blair, which disempowered governments and disenfranchised voters, was a political choice made by successive governments. It did not impact other European countries in the same way because they made different policy choices and had different priorities. Dislocation and inequality were not the product of nature; they were the product of political choice.

This meant that, by the end of the New Labour years, the hope that had accompanied his election in the post-industrial towns had dissipated into anger and disenchantment. The promise of renewal hadn't been fulfilled and many towns saw continued decline. Much of Labour's heartland complained about being 'taken for granted' and a number of the forgotten towns had Blairite MPs with little connection to the area parachuted into them. New Labour's style became increasingly technocratic and detached from their once-solid working-class base, with the views of Labour MPs becoming increasingly out of step with working-class voters over a wide range of issues, from the EU to immigration.

Blair reportedly said that the focus of New Labour should be on southern middle-class voters (labelled Mondeo Man) and that traditional Labour voters had 'nowhere else to go'. Many of these voters stopped voting altogether and many others briefly shifted their allegiance to UKIP. The first time for decades these voters had come out in droves was for the EU referendum, when almost the entire Labour Party (at least publicly) supported a Remain vote. These short-term voting movements are, however, less important than the long-term trend, which is that, under New Labour, the party shifted from being a predominantly working-class party to being a predominantly middle-class one. The shift away from its working-class base opens up the potential for a broader political realignment. The changing nature of Labour was only accelerated with Jeremy Corbyn's election as Labour leader.

CORBYNISM AS A BOURGEOIS MOVEMENT

Despite protestations to the contrary, Labour under Jeremy Corbyn has become even more distant from its traditional support, completing a journey that was started, in a very different way, by Tony Blair. Forty-eight per cent of Labour's members now come from the south of England and some 77 per cent are middle class. Under Corbyn, Labour's vote among the professional middle classes (demographic group AB) increased by eleven points from 26 per cent under Ed Miliband to 37 per cent in 2017. His vote among the lower-middle-class demographic also increased by 11 per cent from Ed Miliband's score. The vote among working-class voters also increased under Corbyn, but the vast bulk of his success came from attracting middle-class voters to his new Labour Party. In 1997, Labour's lead among skilled working-class voters was some 23 per cent and was as high as 38 per cent among the unskilled working-class voters. By the time of Corbyn's 'success' in 2017, Labour trailed the Tories by 4 per cent among the skilled working class and only led among unskilled working-class voters by 9 per cent. Parties of the left are having to rely on the votes of middle-class voters, which is a development described by Thomas Piketty as the rise of the 'Brahmin left'.

As Bagehot in *The Economist* argued, the working class that Corbyn imagines he is a champion of 'is a working class of his imagination rather than of the real world. He was brought up in a manor house in Shropshire and has spent his life working as an MP in a constituency (Islington North) that has never been touched by either industrialisation or de-industrialisation.' For Bagehot, Corbyn's Labour is dominated by 'three groups: ethnic minorities, particularly Muslims; public-sector professionals; and frustrated millennials, most of them the university-educated children of the salaried middle class'. In this environment, working-class voters who vote for the party out of family loyalty 'are increasingly voting for a party that is no longer "theirs" … They are outsiders lending support, rather than stake-holders exercising ownership.'

Research by the Sutton Trust shows that in 1997, 66 per cent of Labour MPs had been to university. By 2017, this had increased to 84 per cent, which itself was a 7 per cent increase on the figure at the 2015 election. This is despite the fact that the vast majority of school leavers in working-class towns don't tend to attend university. Only 1.5 per cent of Labour MPs were previously employed in manual work, compared with almost 10 per cent who were lawyers, 10 per cent who had been trade union officials, and 12 per cent who had come from the voluntary sector.

This stark divide is also felt across a wide range of issues. Take

Brexit as one. Some 60 per cent of Labour constituencies voted Leave. The skilled working class voted to leave by 24 per cent, and 64 per cent of unskilled working-class voters opted to leave the EU, meaning that Leave won that social group by a clear twenty-eight points. By contrast, only eleven Labour MPs backed Leave in the referendum campaign.

A similar divide can be seen on the issue of immigration, where most Labour MPs back free movement and open borders. Over two thirds of working-class voters told YouGov in 2018 that immigration has been too high over the past ten years and only 17 per cent of these voters said that the level of immigration had been good for the country.

The policy priorities of the Labour Party also reflect the priorities of the middle class, rather than the priorities of its traditional working-class base. Its two flagship policies remain nationalisation of the railways and the abolition of tuition fees. Both of these policies have attractions in their own right, but the fact that they have been chosen as priorities illustrates a great deal about the makeup of the party.

Take tuition fees as an example. Few would disagree that they are too high, but the question remains whether the cost of around £100 billion to abolish fees should be a domestic priority. This is particularly the case given that university attendance remains primarily a middle-class move. Only around a fifth of young people from the most disadvantaged areas go on to higher education. For the one third of most selective universities, 23 per cent of young people from state schools who took A Levels attended the most selective one third of universities, compared to 64 per cent of young people from independent schools. The policy would also have the inevitable impact of enhancing the importance of university at the expense of vocational education, which could continue to be to the detriment of the economy overall and 'left-behind' towns in particular.

A Labour Party that was a genuine champion for the working class would surely prefer to invest money in providing first-class schools in poorer areas and delivering a vocational revolution of the kind I will discuss in the closing chapter. Instead, they effectively choose to prioritise a fiscal transfer from working-class people who are less likely to attend university to middle-class people who do.

The same could be said for nationalisation of the railways. The vast majority of people who commute by rail are in the south-east of England and are generally middle class. Most people elsewhere commute either by car or by bus. Prioritising nationalisation, whatever its merits or otherwise, would again represent a tax subsidy for middle-class voters at the expense of working-class people.

The Labour Party that was strong and dominant around Consett for so long is sadly symbolic of a Labour Party that no longer exists. Its combination of patriotism, economic reform and an emphasis on social cohesion and the interests of working-class voters would have been a powerful and important force to address the problems the country is facing today.

When Herbert Morrison said that Labour shouldn't join the embryonic Common Market because the 'Durham miners won't wear it', he was making a clear statement that the party would revere the views of working-class voters. Now some Labour members and MPs seem to view the attitudes of those voters with little to no respect – as was seen in the aftermath of the Brexit vote.

Sadly, today's Labour Party no longer represents the members of my family who grew up revering it in Consett. It is now fundamentally a middle-class party, representing middle-class interests, with a strong streak of identity liberalism. The implications for British politics of this shift are quite profound. It means that a Tory Party prepared to think beyond economic liberalism and offer hope to long-forgotten towns could build a new and enduring electoral coalition.

CHAPTER EIGHT

REVIVING ONE NATION: A WAY FORWARD?

Our political opponents seem to me to be living either in the past or in a world of make-believe. The pure doctrine of laissez-faire ... [or] the nationalisation of all the means of production, distribution and exchange – these were the cries of my boyhood. What a musty period flavour they have now. How utterly out of touch all this is with the problems and opportunities of today.

– Harold Macmillan

In a progressive country change is constant; and the great question is, not whether you should resist change which is inevitable, but whether that change should be carried out in deference to the manners, the customs, the laws, the traditions of the people, or in deference to abstract principles and arbitrary and general doctrines.

– Benjamin Disraeli

THE SLOW RISE AND RAPID DECLINE OF ONE NATION TORYISM

From the rise of Disraeli until the 1980s, One Nation conservatism was the dominant, and most successful, mode of thinking in British politics. Disraeli himself traced the tradition back to Bolingbroke in the early part of the eighteenth century (as did Rab Butler).

Post 1981, it has rapidly diminished in importance. To many, conservatism is now shorthand for some form of economic liberalism, or even libertarianism. As I have argued, it is clear that such a narrow approach to politics is no longer serving the interests of the economy and is also not serving the Tory Party electorally. Rediscovering One Nation is essential if Conservatives want to be able to take advantage of a profound change in voter behaviour and party loyalties.

Conservatives need to step back from a myopic economic liberalism and consider the deeper, more relevant and more profound elements of conservatism. Only by recapturing this tradition can Conservatives say they have as much to offer to people in Consett as they have in Tunbridge Wells. Only then can they genuinely tackle the issues facing the country.

Some of today's proponents of 'One Nation conservatism' seem remarkably detached from the thinking that gave rise to the phrase. To many, 'One Nation' seems like Thatcherite economics with some corporate social responsibility or liberal social thinking attached. Others throw the phrase around like a buzzword without any consideration of its meaning or derivation. One Nation, however, is an important set of concepts and ideas, including in economics, that deserves to be taken seriously in its own right. One Nation is not, and can never be, merely the political wing of economic liberalism, but, as I will explain, it does understand the importance and wealth-creating power of the market, business and entrepreneurship.

One Nation has a crucial role to play in reuniting two nations between whom there is 'no discourse and no sympathy'. The combination of national unity, economic efficiency and social reform is a potent one in our present degraded circumstances.

WHAT IS ONE NATION?

In order to consider why One Nation is uniquely relevant to our economic, political and social problems, it's important to first gain a better understanding of what One Nation actually is. Even more importantly, we need to understand what it is *not*. Only then can it be used as the basis for a unifying, and successful, policy platform.

I make no apology for drawing on historical examples for part of this chapter. This is for two reasons. The first is that it's important to show that One Nation draws on deep and proud traditions. One Nation has always been able to revive and renew. It is not accidental that British Conservatism is the most successful political tradition in the West, which has managed, despite predictions of doom at the time, to survive multiple party splits, the shift from oligarchy to democracy, the rise and fall of Empire and two world wars. Its flexibility and pragmatism is its great strength, but this is also underpinned by some core, enduring truths.

The second reason is simple and more prosaic. It has been a familiar refrain for people to complain that a certain policy 'isn't really Conservative' or that a politician is a TINO (Tory In Name Only). Remembering the depth of the Tory tradition is a useful rejoinder to the shallowness of this kind of argument and a timely reminder that there was a Tory Party before 1975 and that the Conservative tradition is much deeper than that of pure libertarianism or economic liberalism.

Nevertheless, this is fundamentally a book about practical politics in 2019. Boris Johnson has made clear that he believes in the One Nation tradition and believes that the state must act where necessary, particularly around infrastructure, suggesting that One Nation ideas remain important. My aim has been to make clear how elements of the Tory tradition are more relevant than ever today and how they can be used to drive a fundamental realignment of politics.

A BELIEF IN NATIONAL UNITY

One Nation may well be the only political idea to start from a belief in a fundamental national unity, rather than a country divided by class or sectional interests. In our divided kingdom, an ideology that aims for unity rather than division has much to recommend it.

Lord Hailsham argued in 1959 that this belief in national unity made Tories stand out from their opponents:

> The Conservative Party is based on its love of country ... Conservatism derives its inspiration and seeks to base its policy on

what Conservatives believe to be the underlying unity of all classes
of Englishmen, their ultimate identity of interest, their profound
similarity of outlook, the common dangers and difficulties they
have shared in the past, and with which they are still faced, and the
necessity for unity as the true means for meeting them together ...
Harmony, not struggle, is its ruling political objective.

Tories have long argued that their political opponents were too
keen to see themselves as representatives of one particular element
of society. The nineteenth-century Liberals were representatives
of the capitalist class and modern socialists have been portrayed
only as representatives of one element within society. One Nation
rejects the class division that dominates socialist thinking and
the narrow view of 'economic man' that shaped liberal political
thought. Instead, it sees citizens as belonging to an organic community, with responsibilities and motivations beyond the purely
economic. From the belief in unity flows a determination that
no part of the country should be left behind. One Nation conservatism has no wish to see or preside over two nations. This
often came from personal experience – for example, what Disraeli witnessed while researching his condition-of-England novels
and what Macmillan saw while serving in the First World War
and when MP for Stockton during the Great Depression. Unity
means that certain parts of the country shouldn't benefit at the
expense of others and that government has a duty to do something to help create a united country. This is driven by the belief
that we are part of a broader community, with wider and deeper
responsibilities beyond pure self-interest.

As Disraeli put it in the early 1860s:

The Tory party is only in its proper position when it represents popular principles. Then it is truly irresistible. Then it can uphold the throne and the altar, the majesty of the empire, the liberty of the nation, and the rights of the multitude. There is nothing mean, petty, or exclusive, about the real character of Toryism. It necessarily depends upon enlarged sympathies and noble aspirations, because it is essentially national.

A belief in national unity was shared by Stanley Baldwin during his premiership. He said that, 'for fourteen years I preached up and down Great Britain, attempting to achieve a national unity of spirit and a high conception of what democracy may be, and calling for unselfish service to that ideal'.

The belief that the Tory Party 'is a national party or it is nothing' is often quoted, but seldom genuinely understood. It doesn't necessarily mean that the Tory Party should be the party of Last Night of the Proms-style flag-waving. Rather, it reflects the belief that the party should speak for the whole nation, rather than just sectional interests, and that this national unity brings with it a series of responsibilities. As Lord Hugh Cecil argued, part of loving one's country is realising the need to make one's country lovely.

Nevertheless, this patriotism shouldn't be ignored. One Nation remembers the importance of collective memory in patriotism and respects it as a powerful, progressive force to bring people together, both in peacetime and when going through periods of trauma. This love of country should be a unifying and positive force, which is more important than the divisive politics of class, or more recent variations of identity politics.

This emphasis on unity speaks to a politics that has become deeply divided and polarised. A glance at the angry politics of the USA, with its deep and widening geographic, economic, racial and political divisions, represents a warning of what our politics might become if the divides accentuated by Brexit are allowed to fester and to grow. Equally, political priorities of recent years, as we've set out in earlier chapters, have created a more atomised, less cohesive society. One Nation's emphasis on national unity doesn't represent a healing panacea, but, combined with an ambition to reunite a divided country after several turbulent years, it represents the only sustainable way forward to healing national divisions.

TRUST THE PEOPLE

That the people should be trusted was one of the hallmarks of Disraeli's 'education' of his party. When defending the 1867 Reform Act, he correctly argued that the Act was founded

> on a confidence that the great body of the people of this country were 'Conservative'. I use the word in its purest and loftiest sense. I mean that the people of England, and especially the working classes of England, are proud of belonging to a great country, and wish to maintain its greatness ... There are people who may be, or who at least affect to be, working men, and who, no doubt, have a certain influence with a certain portion of the metropolitan working class, who talk Jacobinism ... I say with confidence that the

great body of the working class of England utterly repudiate such sentiments. They have no sympathy with them. They are English to the core. They repudiate cosmopolitan principles. They adhere to national principles.

It was Lord Randolph Churchill who carried on the message of 'trusting the people' after the death of Disraeli. In the mid-1880s, he implored: 'Governments will go wrong, Parliaments will go wrong, classes will go wrong, London society and the Pall Mall clubs will go wrong, but the people do not go wrong.'

Disraeli's trust in the British people certainly seems to have been borne out. Although many predicted that Conservatism would be the big loser from the onset of democracy, it actually became the big winner, with British Conservatives proving electorally dominant in the democratic age. This was to confound the predictions of the unlikely duo of Karl Marx and Lord Salisbury. Marx argued that universal suffrage would be 'a far more socialistic measure than anything which has been honoured with that name on the continent. Its inevitable result, here, is the political supremacy of the working class.' Salisbury, meanwhile, regarded universal suffrage as a disaster for Conservatism, arguing that 'the Conservative Party [has] dealt themselves a fatal blow by the course which they have adopted.'

It was the Conservatives who went on to dominate most of the 150 years following the 1867 Reform Act, and Salisbury, as Prime Minister at various times between 1885 and 1902, was one of the main beneficiaries. A mixture of patriotism and social reform proved to be attractive to working-class voters. Friedrich

Engels displayed his frustration when he said: 'Once again the proletariat has discredited itself terribly ... It cannot be denied that the increase of working class voters has brought the Tories more than their simple percentage increase; it has improved their relative position.' By contrast, since their formation, the Labour Party has only had three leaders who have won working majorities in general elections.

Although, as we've seen, messaging, leadership and policy have changed dramatically, what has been at the heart of British Conservatism since Disraeli's time is an instinctive faith and trust in the British people. This has been accompanied with a desire to empower the people as much as possible: not only through democratic norms, but also by making sure that as many people as possible are able to benefit from share ownership, homeownership and low rates of tax (trusting the people to decide how to spend their own money). Conservatism is also more likely to trust ordinary people with decisions over their lives than placing, as the abstract left does, too much faith in the hands of distant bureaucrats.

In an age of abstract internationalism, trusting the people, including those in disengaged communities such as Consett, is more important than ever. Its relevance, however, goes well beyond that. As we have seen, a central element of modern discontent is the fact that many, particularly in the forgotten towns, believe that they have lost agency and control as part of today's economic and political settlement. Equally, much of modern politics consists of patronising the people, effectively telling them that they can't think for themselves regarding diet and health. Remembering the 'trust the people' motto must be a fundamental element of a modern political programme.

BELIEF IN THE MARKET ECONOMY

As will be discussed, Conservatives have never had the blind faith in laissez-faire that liberals have – they see that as hopelessly utopian. Conservatism does, however, believe strongly that private enterprise and the market economy is, by some way, the best means to create wealth and prosperity. No better way has ever been found to create and share prosperity, and Conservatives believe in championing and supporting the market mechanism as a proven creator of prosperity. They understand that without this wealth and prosperity the support for the poorest, also an essential part of One Nation, would be much more difficult to provide and sustain, but also believe that this market economy should be moored in cultural and societal norms.

One Nation Conservatives believe that entrepreneurship and risk-taking are to be encouraged. They believe in fair taxation, but don't believe that this taxation should be set at a level that discourages the kind of risk-taking that is needed to drive the economy forward.

One Nation also believes in a genuinely popular capitalism, where small businesses are given the freedom to prosper. One Nation believes that economic power is best dispersed as widely as possible and that the widespread ownership of both property and capital is an effective way to achieve this. This is why Conservatives have always believed that homeownership is a good thing and property rights must be respected. In this, Margaret Thatcher was continuing in the long tradition of a 'property-owning de-mocracy', an idea first articulated by Noel Skelton in the 1920s and repeated by One Nation leaders afterwards.

Crucially, this is paired with a belief that property comes with responsibility. Macmillan made this clear in his 1938 *The Middle Way* when he said that the 'object of all our endeavours must be to lift the burdens of poverty and distress that weigh so heavily upon great masses of the people, in order to build up a secure and adequate standard of life for all'. Conservatives have a strong faith in liberty and freedom but do not believe that this can be restrict-ed to economic freedom for the already wealthy. As Macmillan put it, this must also include 'liberty from the humiliation and restraints of unnecessary poverty; liberty from any unnecessary burden of toil; liberty from the haunting fear of insecurity'.

At their best, Conservatives are supportive of business without being a pressure group for business. They are quite ready to call out abuses where they occur and always stand up for the citizen and the consumer. Conservatives are clear that the market mech-anism represents by far the best way of allocating resources and generating wealth. Where they differ from liberals, however, is in the belief that the market doesn't always work perfectly and that the state has a role and a responsibility to act when the market is not working effectively.

They see that the trend of the market isn't towards what the laissez-faire thinkers would have described as 'perfect competition'; rather they see that the market, when left unchecked, tends towards domination and a lack of competition. As Adam Smith famous-ly said: 'People of the same trade seldom meet together, even for merriment and diversion, but the conversation ends in a conspiracy against the public, or in some contrivance to raise prices.'

Conservatives subscribe to Acton's nostrum that 'power tends to corrupt and absolute power corrupts absolutely.' As such, they are instinctively unwilling to allow too much power to concentrate in one place, whether that be in the state, in the City of London, in trade unions or in dominant corporations. Conservatism looks to take on vested interests wherever they may be. This means looking to maintain competition with strong competition authorities and always remaining vigilant that the interest of the citizen and consumer is protected.

This is more relevant now than ever. Conservatives must be ready to make the case for the market mechanism at the same time as a new generation of hipster socialists stand ready to turn back most of its gains. Conservatives, as opposed to uncritical economic liberals, also need to stand ready to ensure that the benefits of business are felt by all workers, rather than just those at the top, and that the basic elements are in place to ensure that all parts of the country are able to benefit from the job- and prosperity-creating engine of capitalism.

AN ACTIVE AND INTELLIGENT STATE

Whereas liberals have traditionally been distrustful of the state and authority, Tories have been more inclined to see it as a potential force for good in order to preserve national unity. This has meant that Conservatism has traditionally believed in the power of the state and has been distrustful of the simplistic nature of laissez-faire. Disraeli memorably said that

Liberal opinions are the opinions of those who would be free from certain constraints and regulations, from a certain dependence and duty which are deemed necessary for the general or popular welfare. Liberal opinions are very convenient opinions for the rich and powerful. They ensure enjoyment and are opposed to self-sacrifice.

Lord Hugh Cecil put it slightly differently in his turn-of-the-century consideration of 'Conservatism':

It is often assumed that Conservatism and Socialism are directly opposed. But that is not completely true. Modern Conservatism inherits the traditions of Toryism which are favourable to the activity and authority of the State. Indeed, Mr Herbert Spencer attacked Socialism as in fact the revival of Toryism.

Rab Butler argued that 'Conservatives have always been ready to use the power of the state. That has been our tradition since Bolingbroke.' Conservatism is not about opposition to state action. Instead, it is about using the power of the state to promote the common good. It was Tories, for example, who believed most deeply in the local poor law that was swept away in the Whigs' Poor Law Reform (which Disraeli described as 'disgracing the nation'). As Tombs set out:

The reality is more complex, and more intriguing [than the modern caricature of Toryism]. For example, reactionary 'High Tory' beliefs – state intervention to defend the vulnerable, high spending on welfare, rejection of deflationary economics – chime more with modern sentiments than those of the progressive Whigs – rigid economic determinism, tax cuts, harsh welfare restrictions.

A key part of the organic theory of the state is the Tory belief that the state should represent all of its people and the state should have the power to benefit all of its people. Because of this, Toryism had little truck with Unitarianism, homo economicus and the crude simplicities of laissez-faire. It also makes One Nation particularly suited to addressing the problems of today, which require sensible use of the state to address clear issues, while also not allowing the reach of the state to become suffocating.

This has been seen in practice from Disraeli's time through to the present day. The record of Benjamin Disraeli's government on social reform was impressive. Slum clearance, the improvement of working-class housing, Public Health Acts, a Factory Act, the legalisation of picketing and laws that allowed workers to sue employers if a contract was broken all provided a firm basis for the nascent Tory tradition of social reform. Disraeli's slum clearance programmes and wide-ranging social reform led a trade union leader of the day to commend that the 'Conservatives have done more for the working class in seven years than the liberals did in seventy.'

Disraeli created a tradition that showed that it was the responsibility of Toryism to use the power and authority of the state to tackle poverty and improve conditions for working people. It is this tradition that must be revived today in order to tackle the lingering social issues that follow on from deindustrialisation and the social problems of poverty and homelessness that provide an increasingly visible scar on our major cities.

One Nation Toryism never fell for the simplicity of market liberalism. As Hailsham argued:

> The liberals of the nineteenth century proclaimed a jihad against all forms of ... interference in the realm of commerce ... The laws of supply and demand were far more just and infinitely wiser than the most cunningly contrived regulations of potentates or their Ministers ... The Conservatives, as always out of date, did not quite believe them ... It was the Tory Party which stood in the nineteenth century against the principles of laissez faire Liberalism ... For the remedy proposed by Disraeli ... was as entirely up to date as his analysis of the disease. The privileges of the multitude could only be safeguarded by an increase in the executive power of government.

After Disraeli's death, some of the wind was removed from the sails of radical Toryism. Randolph Churchill, with his compelling concept of Tory Democracy, was able to create the Primrose League, which had more working-class members in its heyday than the Labour Party. Lord Randolph was to prove to be a firework who fizzled out too quickly but, as his biographer Robert Rhodes-James made clear, he left a legacy, which is still important today, when the intricate dogmas of both left and right are gaining ground:

> There has always been in modern England a body of opinion which cannot be reconciled to Reaction or Radicalism; this body

believes in social progress, and yet for a variety of reasons cannot stomach the intricate dogmas of the Left. It was to this ... that ... Tory Democracy appealed so strongly.

Although the Baldwin and Chamberlain years were marred by a failure to address unemployment and will be for ever judged by their policies of appeasement, they did broaden the activities of the state in a number of ways. Old-age pensions were extended, the state took steps to modernise industry and the old doctrine of free trade and laissez-faire was replaced with a more pragmatic approach designed to help industry, rather than fit within a dogmatic code. Baldwin argued that 'the Conservative Party regards the prosperity of trade and industry, not as an end in itself, but as a means to improve the condition of the people.' Lord Lexden, the Conservative historian, argued that

[Baldwin] committed it to the task of healing Britain's deep social divide. He struck the note which was to reverberate throughout subsequent Tory (and indeed British) history in a speech on 4 December 1924. He said: 'we stand for the union of those two nations of which Disraeli spoke two generations ago: union among our own people to make One Nation of our own people at home which, if secured, nothing else matters in the world'.

Lexden continued:

Local government services were transformed, large swathes of slums were cleared and over two million new homes built, contributory pensions were introduced and the first national health services were provided as a result of the initiatives of the inspired social reformer [Neville Chamberlain] who worked at Baldwin's side in giving practical expression to his vision of one nation.

Post-war Conservative governments also had few qualms about using the state to improve the lives of citizens. Despite the critique of some right-wing commentators, Churchill understood that there needed to be domestic change after the war was won. In 1940, he said in a speech to his old school, Harrow, that the aim for the post-war period should be to 'establish a state of society where the advantages and privileges which have hitherto been enjoyed only by the few shall be far more widely shared by the many'. In 1943, he made clear that he was a 'strong partisan' of 'national compulsory insurance for all classes for all purposes from the cradle to the grave'. As part of this, he felt that his government's policy should 'create a national health service in order to ensure that everybody in the country, irrespective of means, age, sex, or occupation, shall have equal opportunities to benefit from the best and most up-to-date medical and allied services available'.

It should be remembered that the social reforms of the Attlee government were, in many ways, a continuation of the efforts of the coalition government, of which many of the most distinguished of the 1945 government had also been members. As Paul Addison pointed out: 'The Coalition proved to be the greatest reforming administration since the Liberal government of 1905–1914.' He wrote: 'Social Security for all, family allowances, major reform in education, a National Health Service, Keynesian budgetary techniques, town and country planning, closer relations between the state and industry – all these had been set on foot by the spring of 1943.' In 1944, Churchill had reaffirmed this, telling the Commons that 'all the leading men in both principal parties are pledged and committed to this great mass of social legislation, and I cannot conceive that, whatever may be the complexion of the new House, they will personally fail to make good their promises and commitments to the people.'

Macmillan's memories of the sufferings of Stockton during the Depression never left him and infused his philosophy. In his first conference speech as Prime Minister, he said:

> There may be some people – there must be in this audience – young enough not to have known, there may be some so remote from reality not to realise what mass unemployment involves in human suffering. Certainly, anyone of my age, or who has had my experience, can never put it out of his mind. We do not seek unemployment – we seek to avert it. And if it ever comes to the people of this country again, it can only come in one way: it will be a self-inflicted wound.

Famously, Macmillan, while Housing Minister and Prime Minister, used the power of the state to pursue one of the most ambitious housebuilding strategies in the Western world.

It's easy to write off Macmillan as the fusty product of the grouse fields or as that great 'actor manager', but that is not what can be seen in the fascinating political economy of *The State and Industry* or *The Middle Way*, or indeed in the way in which he governed over six ambitious years. Equally, it would be easy to re-member him for the failed attempt at Common Market member-ship, the grotesque nonsense of Beeching and the butchery of the railways or the sordidness of Profumo. That is not, however, how we should think about him today. Instead, we should remember the words of former Labour Minister and founder member of the SDP David Marquand, who confessed to being surprised at thinking that Macmillan, 'that master of irony and specialist in ambiguity, emerges from my story as the nearest thing to a great Prime Minister in the post-war period'.

He was probably the last Prime Minister with a genuine belief in 'Toryism' and the real importance of balancing economic efficien-cy with social justice. He had a burning desire that we must never again become 'two nations' and was convinced that government and private enterprise had an important role to play, together, in preventing that from happening. He believed in modernising industry and the country, but without the managerial indifference of Heathism or the retreat into liberal economic determinism. His One Nation was a profound belief in the common good and the fundamental national unity that makes us stronger.

Although the Thatcher and Major governments were elected on a platform of shrinking the state, the evidence of their use of the state can be seen in places like Canary Wharf and Liverpool. Economic liberalism became a guiding light from the late 1970s, but neither Thatcher nor Major lost faith in the importance of the state managing welfare or health care. Sadly, their relative lack of interest in the state promoting research or innovation was to have a deleterious impact on British industry over the longer term.

Throughout its history, One Nation has shown a willingness to use the power of the state to elevate the condition of the people. Boris Johnson's stated desire to use the state to build the infrastructure that our regions need is a clear continuation of this tradition. Such an intelligent use of the state to empower people who feel that they have lost agency should be the order of the day now as much as it was a century ago. As I'll set out, the state has a fundamental role to play in ensuring that forgotten towns have the infrastructure than enables them to grow and prosper in a way that they haven't in recent decades.

CONTINUITY

A partnership in all science, a partnership in all art, a partnership in every virtue and in all perfection. As the ends of such a partnership cannot be obtained in many generations, it becomes a partnership not only between those who are living, but between those who are living, those who are dead, and those who are to be born.

This was the unforgettable way in which Edmund Burke summarised the importance of continuity to the One Nation creed. This belief in continuity, for both community and country, is a fundamental element of One Nation. We are not as we are because of chance; this continuity is a fundamental part of who we are and the country and community in which we exist. Conservatives don't believe in Hayek's 'movement for movement's sake' or a free market that is detached from societal or cultural mooring. This is nicely put by Quintin Hogg in his *Conservative Case*. He argues that

Conservatives believe that this store of wisdom is not something fixed and unalterable which we have received from our ancestors but a treasury to which it is the duty of each generation to make its characteristic contribution. But it follows from this that Conservatives reject any of the various 'Copernican' or revolutionary theories of politics ... They do not believe that each generation in turn should start from scratch, abandoning all the wisdom; on the contrary, they consider that progress consists in each generation beginning at the point where their fathers left off. If we acted as if progress consisted in scrapping the achievements of the past, Conservatives do not think we should get very far.

He goes on to say that human community:

is much more like a living being than a machine or a house ... human societies have individualities. These are ultimately indefinable ... The Conservative theory of the individuality of human societies cuts at the root of the left-wing theories of an 'ideal state' or an 'ideal man' ... Perfection in human societies or human individuals no more means that everyone should be alike than that perfection in horticulture would involve that all gardens should be built on one pattern growing flowers of identical size and colour. The theory of individuality involves an understanding of individual tradition, proclivities and requirements. We do not necessarily grow more like one another as we grow better.

This is allied to the belief in national unity and in the best of patriotism. One Nation might see that the monarchy seems odd to the literal observer (Joseph Chamberlain described himself as a republican in theory but not in practice), but understands that monarchy embodies the continuity that has made Britain into the country it is today. Our institutions might not be perfect, but they are certainly special. In this, One Nation might be romantic, but this romanticism strikes a chord with the people that laissez-faire and miserabilist socialism simply doesn't. Witness the excitement that accompanied the Jubilees and the royal weddings (some 26 million people watched the wedding of the Duke and Duchess of Cambridge). Only the One Nation conservative can understand that the power of this lies in the instinctive understanding of continuity between past, present and future in the hearts of the British people.

The British Parliament may have its faults, but even a casual observer would accept that it represents an institution that is special, that clearly stands as a monument to this continuity. Barry and Pugin designed a palace whose gothic architecture and its soaring, ethereal qualities reflected man's desire to strive to do better. It was decorated internally with murals and statues which evoked defining moments of our ancestors, major national events that told the story of the struggle for British liberty. The paintings by William Dyce in the Robing Room illustrate the chivalric virtues of hospitality, generosity, mercy, religion and courtesy – aspects of virtue that could be rallied around by all. With the central lobby decorated with 1920s mosaics of the patron saints of England, Wales, Scotland and Ireland, it aimed to embody a vision of what it is to be British.

Even that arch liberal, Tony Blair, described the House of Commons as an arena 'that makes the heart beat a little faster'.

Part of its charm is in the fact that we know the great battles of the past have occurred in this chamber, where Fox battled Pitt, where Disraeli outwitted Gladstone, where Arthur Greenwood was encouraged to 'speak for England, Arthur', and where Churchill bewitched the British people with oratory and encouraged a weak-kneed establishment to carry on fighting tyranny. The statues that circle the central lobby – the foot of Churchill gone pale from rubbing for good luck, the memories of Lloyd George, Attlee, Disraeli and Macmillan – all bear testament to an institution that has not sprung from nothing.

Bevan criticised these statues as representing 'ancestor worship', whereas the One Nation Conservative understands that such veneration merely respects the fact that the present generation has not accumulated perfect knowledge and that wisdom comes from a respect of the past, rather than a desire to destroy it. If Britain adopted a horseshoe legislature, took away the statues and the pictures and embraced a 'forward-looking consensus', it is hard for a Tory to consider what would be gained, but easy to be starkly alarmed at the tradition that would be lost.

This is summed up by Sir Roger Scruton's identification, going back to Burke, that 'good things are easily destroyed, but not so easily created', and that preserving a store of wisdom through the ages is preferable to the destruction of that store and the prevalent belief that this generation somehow has a monopoly on such knowledge.

Burke articulated this belief in continuity when he said that an

idea of a liberal descent inspires us with a sense of habitual native dignity ... By this means our liberty becomes a noble freedom.

It carries an imposing and majestic aspect. It has a pedigree and illustrating ancestors. It has its bearings and its ensigns armorial. It has its gallery of portraits; its monumental inscriptions; its record, evidence and titles.

He wrote to a French correspondent that he might

have profited of our example ... You might have repaired those walls; you might have built on those old foundations [yet] you chose to act as if you had never been moulded into civic society, and had everything to begin anew. You began ill, because you began by despising everything that belonged to you.

One Nation, of course, also understands that this belief in continuity and a golden thread cannot and must not stop at political institutions. The country as a whole stands as an example of continuity and preservation. Hundreds of thousands of racing fans turn up at the increasingly popular Cheltenham Festival every year, prepared to indulge in Guinness and revelry, but also in their own form of ancestor worship. The Arkle Bar celebrates the Gold Cup's greatest champion, and fans, born several decades after the great steeplechaser, still whisper his name with awe. The Durham Miners' Gala is dominated by the spirit (and the banners) of those who have gone and sacrificed before. Again, it is this golden thread that conservatives understand and liberals do not.

One must not suggest that politics should get lost in hopeless romanticism. One Nation's belief in continuity does, however, have substantial importance to a politics that is relevant in 2019.

It emphasises the importance of conservation and environmental awareness within Conservatism. It also identifies the importance of a Conservatism that isn't so hopelessly attracted to constant, remorseless change and is more supportive of those institutions, such as family, community and nation, that represent continuity with the past and inheritance of the future.

A DISTRUST OF DOGMA AND A
HATRED OF ABSTRACT IDEOLOGIES

One Nation also believes, in stark contrast to many of today's economic liberals and doctrinaire socialists, that ideological certainty and systems are bad things. All too often, they are driven by a strident certainty that a simplistic ideology has the answer to all of today's problems. As Hailsham said:

> The whole assumption that it is possible to sum up human political needs in one of a series of catchwords strikes the mind as impossibly naive. Nothing is more certain than that the latest ideas of one age are hopelessly dated or outmoded in the next, and Conservatives prefer to subject the 'spirit of the age' to a certain amount of honest scepticism in the light of their knowledge that each political nostrum will appear to succeeding generations as a dangerous and outmoded fallacy.

What One Nation is not, of course, is a dogmatic faith in one type of government or system or another. Indeed, that is one of the things that differentiates it from the rigidity of market liberalism or dogmatic socialism. Conservatism maintains a healthy scepticism of man-made utopias. It remembers that the graves of millions were buried under utopian attempts of the twentieth century and that the misery of the 'wail of intolerable serfage' was created by another utopia in the nineteenth century.

Lord Hailsham writes that 'other parties may be wedded to fixed and unalterable theories of the state [but] the Conservative Party is not. Its eternal and indispensable role is to criticise and mould the latest heresy of the moment in the name of tradition, as tradition itself has been enriched and moulded by the transient theories of the past.' Conservatives reject abstract theories or systems which ignore the relevance of cultural circumstances. As such, they reject abstractions, whether they emerge from the pen of Karl Marx, Jean Jacques-Rousseau or Friedrich Von Hayek. As Michael Oakeshott, one of the most important twentieth-century British Tory thinkers, argued, Hayek's plan 'to resist all planning may be better than the opposite, but it belongs to the same style of politics'. Tories were rightly sceptical of the destructiveness inherent in Marxism and the Jacobin doctrines before it, arguing that although they were clear about what they wanted to destroy and about what a utopia might look like, they were notably much less clear about what should happen between the destruction and the utopia.

Just as they have proven sceptical of the destructive utopianism of socialism, Conservatives have also taken utopian liberalism to task. They regarded von Mises's assertion that mankind had a clear choice between Soviet Communism and laissez-faire as an utterly ridiculous one. Hayek failed to notice the difference between social reform and full-throated socialism, and thought that theories could be applied universally, whereas Conservatives are keen to consider the importance of national experience. In a memorable passage, Ian Gilmour points out the incoherence of Hayek's attack on Conservatism:

> Most of [Hayek's] charges against Conservatism are merely pejorative descriptions of attributes in which Conservatives take pride. Thus what to Hayek is opportunism, is to Conservatives paying proper attention to circumstances. What Hayek calls the use of arbitrary power, the Conservative calls the legitimate use of the power of the state to promote the welfare of the people. What to Hayek is the Conservative inability to offer an alternative direction, is to Conservatives a concern to preserve the stability, unity and continuity of the country and the realisation that violent upheavals or ideological strife threaten the fabric of society – and also, incidentally, weaken the hold of liberal ideas and values … while Hayek complains of Conservative inability to produce a political philosophy, the Conservative points to the dangerous and unconservative nature of systems of political thought.

Burke argued that Conservatives should distrust abstract theories or 'hocus pocus'. He explained this by saying: 'I mean always a weak, erroneous, fallacious, unfounded or imperfect theory; and one of the ways of ensuring that it is false theory is by comparing it with practice.'

For One Nation, Marxism and laissez-faire are both abstract theories, based on mistaken assumptions, which are generally found wanting by real-world experience. Crucially, for Burke and those who followed him, imposing abstract ideas can never work because of the importance of 'circumstance' and culture. Thus, for One Nation, economics cannot be imposed and must always be culturally and practically relevant. As Macmillan put it: 'Instead of working downwards from the realms of abstract theory, we shall work upwards from the needs of mankind to the complicated economic and social organisation necessary to supply those needs.'

While Prime Minister in the 1960s, Harold Macmillan was able to mock the ideological certainties and 'purity' of his opponents, which marked them out from his One Nation conservatism:

> Our political opponents seem to me to be living either in the past or in a world of make-believe. The pure doctrine of laissez-faire and absolute free trade; the nationalisation of all the means of production, distribution and exchange – these were the cries of my boyhood. What a musty period flavour they have now. How utterly out of touch all this is with the problems and opportunities of today.

This has never been more relevant than in 2019. On the left, politicians who have spent most of their careers associating with far-left Marxist sects once again espouse the same far-left doctrines that have failed and been rejected so many times in the past. On the right, doctrinaires are again pushing for the 'pure doctrine of laissez-faire'. Conservatives would be wise to listen to Macmillan's words. In doing so, they should reject the politics of 'the past or in a world of make believe'. Instead, they should look to position themselves as a compassionate alternative to utopian extremes. Unlike these extremes, One Nation is particularly well placed to tackle the problems faced today.

A BELIEF IN BALANCE AND A DISTRUST
OF TOP-DOWN SOCIALISM

If there is one Tory belief, it is that no institution should gain absolute power. Whigs and liberals see the market as somehow divine and are prepared to give it power that surpassed the common good and general welfare. Tories reject this. Tories also reject the idea that government can be all-seeing or all-knowing, and certainly reject the concept that government should own all and control all, believing that this contains the seeds of a destruction of freedom and diversity. Therefore, they reject utopian socialism as emphatically as they reject laissez-faire liberalism.

Tories believe that excessive state power is damaging both to the national economy and to the liberty of the citizen. Placing a huge amount of power and control in the national government, through state ownership and socialist planning, diminishes the balance and dispersion of power that is essential to both liberty and prosperity.

An innate scepticism about concentration of power and a belief that absolute power will be abused leads One Nation to look for dispersed authority. A socialist utopia is the antithesis of this approach.

Furthermore, Conservatives are empiricists and can see that any attempt to replace the profit motive with centralised state planning has proven considerably less effective than the market mechanism as a means of allocating goods and services or creating wealth. They don't have to look very far to see clear examples of these failures. It is a reasonable rule of thumb that any country that people are prepared to risk their life in order to leave is not a success story. The attempt to build a socialist utopia in East Germany culminated in authorities having to construct a wall to keep their own citizens from leaving. Today, the failed state of Venezuela, despite being the most oil-rich country in the world, has been reduced by a socialist experiment to seeing its people starving and risking their lives to escape.

There is no system of wealth creation that comes close to the market mechanism for creating wealth and producing the goods that society needs. One Nation understands, however, that this is not a zero-sum concept, and that some state involvement, through a mixed economy, can help to maximise the benefits of the market mechanism in many areas. They believe that private property is an important guarantor of freedom and, equally, is crucial in building up a sense of community and belonging. They also believe, however, that the right to own property should also be accompanied by responsibilities that come with property ownership.

Conservatives do not believe in the untrammelled power of the market, and neither do they believe in the untrammelled power of the state. Macmillan drew upon the concept of achieving balance in his conference speeches. In 1960, he argued:

Last century when Liberalism was in the ascendancy, Conservatives felt the need to counteract the excess of individualism and
laissez-faire. When we came into office in 1951, we found that the
balance had been upset in the other direction – too much power
concentrated in the State ... Too much State control endangers
freedom and initiative; but a free-for-all exalts rights over duties

and means that the weak go to the wall. Extremes undermine the national unity which it is our Conservative tradition to foster ... Our aim is to harmonise different and conflicting interests, not to set them against each other with the strident accents of the class war. We aim to balance them so that all can contribute as One Nation to the common good.

As he put it on a separate occasion: 'But while it is and has always been opposed to State domination, the Tory Party has never stood for the sacrifice of human values to the doctrines of a completely free economy. Between Socialism and the old laissez-faire Liberalism there is indeed a Middle Way.'

The Tory case against dogmatic socialism desperately needs to be heard. The old model of statist socialism provides no answer to restoring the dynamism of post-industrial towns. Nor does it help to provide people with agency or control – instead it takes both away from working people. Rather than answering the socialist case with another utopian dogma, Conservatives should call on One Nation principles and respond with ideas that are aimed at tackling the immediate problems of the day.

A DISTRUST OF LAISSEZ-FAIRE AND THE DERIVATION OF THE ONE NATION SYNTHESIS

In many ways, conservatism, and One Nation in particular, rose as the antithesis to the simplicities of laissez-faire and its lack of interest in the general welfare of the people. For One Nation, economics must be grounded in empiricism and culture. The 'laws' of economics aren't metaphysical or natural; they are man-made, and One Nation believes that economics should be used to the benefit of the whole nation, rather than being viewed as a set of unbreakable natural laws.

Macmillan once expressed his delight that the concept of 'an unplanned self-adjusting economic system had been destroyed for ever'. Under Macmillan's direction, a Conservative Central Office paper described laissez-faire as 'an interlude which ended long before the end of the nineteenth century'.

The rise of One Nation partially as a reaction to the dogma of market liberalism is an important aspect of its appeal. Conservatives rightly eschew utopian worldviews and Disraeli memorably described the market society that the Whigs aimed to establish after the Great Reform Act as 'a utopia composed purely of wealth and toil', based on a 'spirit of rapacious covetousness'. The creation of laissez-faire in the nineteenth century was a utopian project created not by the organic nature of society, as Hayek and others suggest, but by the very deliberate legislative acts of the Tory Party's opponents. Laissez-faire was a liberal experiment in utopianism, which the Conservatives rightly condemned and rejected.

As Disraeli surmised, the 'sophisticated theoreticians' of liberalism were able to articulate the theoretical benefits of laissez-faire, but all around them people in England could see and feel that the utopian theories were not delivering utopian results for a great number of the population. He argued that he 'had seen that while immense fortunes were accumulating, while wealth was increasing to a superabundance ... the working classes, the creators of wealth, were steeped in the most abject poverty and gradually sinking into the deepest degradation'. Thus, One Nation was able to develop ideas that rejected the simplistic nostrums of lais-sez-faire and insisted that government could, and indeed should, act to improve the lives of the people.

Disraeli's Crystal Palace speech of 1872 is worth quoting in detail. Not only did it set out the triptych of patriotism, pres-ervation of institutions and social reform that would act as the underpinning for Tory thinking, but it also compellingly laid out the Conservative case against laissez-faire. In the speech, he con-trasted Toryism with Liberalism, emphasising his Tory priority of 'the elevation of the condition of the people'. He emphasised that Toryism understood that 'no important step can be gained unless you can effect some reduction of their hours of labour and hu-manise their toil'. Tories believed that this could be done with 'no injury on the wealth of the nation'. Liberals responded, according to Disraeli, that any measures of social reform that interfered with the market, would result in a 'great diminution of the employ-ment of the people, and ultimately to the impoverishment of the kingdom'. This was the view expressed by (and we can only guess at their identity) 'the most blatant and loud-mouthed leaders of the Liberal Party'. Disraeli was able to look back at the result of the Tory reforms that interfered with the market mechanism (re-forms carried 'with great difficulty and after much labour and a long struggle') and report that, after these reforms, the Liberal warnings were wrong. Instead, 'wages were never higher, that the employment of the people was never greater, and the country never wealthier'.

He used the same speech to declare that

the health of the people was the most important question for a statesman ... It involves the state of the dwellings of the people, the moral consequences of which are not less considerable than the physical. It involves their enjoyment of some of the chief elements of nature – air, light, and water. It involves the regulation of their industry, the inspection of their toil. It involves the purity of their provisions, and it touches upon all the means by which you may wean them from habits of excess and of brutality.

His riposte to Liberals predicting that any action by the state would lead to job losses and ruin could equally have been used as a riposte to modern libertarian warnings about increasing the minimum wage.

To paraphrase David Cameron, the Factory Acts were not introduced despite their proposers being Tories, they were introduced *because* they were Tories. Tories, of course, saw the ability of the market mechanism to increase national wealth, but they also, unlike the Liberals, saw the importance of the power of the state in correcting the imbalances that had been created by utopian laissez-faire. When this balance had been corrected by important social reforms, One Nation started to focus on ensuring that prosperity wasn't stifled by an ill-thought-out socialism.

Thus, the Tory approach has been, and still should be, to seek balance and to reform known injustices and grievances. The liberal route of unbridled laissez-faire was one that produced great wealth, but also great social injustice. The socialist alternative claimed to be able to remedy these social injustices, but also proposed no means of creating wealth and instead merely restricted freedom and concentrated power among the elite.

The Tory balance between the two, or 'synthesis', was to ensure a market system that generated wealth, but in a way in which prosperity was shared and social injustices were tackled. Achieving this balance is more crucial now than ever, when so many believe that the economic and political settlement isn't working for them. It's important that Tories don't look to take on the utopian dogma of socialism with an equally utopian dogma of laissez-faire liberalism. Instead, Tories should look to create a balance that maintains the economic benefits of the market mechanism, but also preserves social cohesion. The Tories also shouldn't be the party that defends all of the rough edges of the market mechanism: low pay, anti-social hours or excessive executive pay. Instead they should look to maintain the dynamism of capitalism, while ironing out its rough edges and ensuring that it works in the interests of the majority in society.

MAN AS A SOCIAL BEING

There are some important similarities between Conservatism and Liberalism, but the key and fundamental difference is that regarding the nature of the individual and the community. It is why conservatism, rather than liberalism, provides an answer to the crisis of atomisation and decline of community feeling that has so heavily impacted modern Britain.

Liberalism sees humanity as defined by their individual needs and individual choices. The primacy of the individual is the central element of liberalism. Conservatism, by contrast, sees the individual as important, but considers the individual as a product of community and society. Man exists as an individual, but he is not complete without his surrounding community and nation. For liberals, individual autonomy is fundamental, whereas, for conservatives, this autonomy can only exist within a defined community and within a complex network of social reciprocity and obligations. Mere self-interest or the satisfaction of personal whims is, for a conservative, not only shallow but can also be detrimental to the good of the community, the nation and, ultimately, the individual himself.

Somebody who has been brought up in France is different to somebody who has been brought up in England not because of differences of individuality, but because of the importance of community, family and the history that flows from and into this. Any ideology that concentrates primarily on the individual, as liberalism does, ignores these crucial elements of human nature. Similarly, any ideology that ignores the individual, family and community, as socialism does, is equally doomed to fail. Only One Nation is developed in accordance with human nature, rather than attempting to distort or shape it.

As Jesse Norman argued when discussing the thought of Edmund Burke:

> The individual is not simply a compendium of wants; human happiness is not simply a matter of satisfying individual wants;

and the purpose of politics is not to satisfy the interests of individuals living now. It is to preserve a social order which addresses the needs of generations past, present and future.

Roger Scruton put this well when considering the complementarities between conservatism and environmental protection:

> Conservatism, as I understand it, means the maintenance of social ecology. It is true that individual freedom is part of that ecology, since without it, social organisms cannot adapt. But freedom is not the only goal of politics. Conservatism and conservation are two aspects of a single long-term policy, which is that of husbanding resources and ensuring their renewal ... Conservatism emphasises historical loyalties, local identities and the kind of long-term commitment that arises amongst people by virtue of their localised and limited affections. While socialism and liberalism are inherently global in their aims, conservatism is inherently local: a defence of some pocket of social capital against the forces of anarchic change.

For Conservatives, there are many natural forms of social organisation, notably family, community and nation. These are the 'little platoons' that Burke referred to, which create a sense of identity and belonging. For the bulk of the population, the nation holds an important and strong emotional attachment, which is instinctively recognised by Conservatives. One Nation recognises that the nation is an important guarantor of stability, security and self-determination in which its citizens hold an emotional connection and a sense of belonging. This is why conservatism must always be a national, rather than an abstract philosophy, because it is rooted in the peculiarities, principles and practices of the nation from which it sprung.

The English have always been a nation of strong towns and villages, and within these villages, strong communal institutions have prospered. These places have had strong local pride and an identity of their own, a strong communal ethos and the kind of historical memory that One Nation also associates with the nation. These have ranged from working men's and social clubs, pubs, village halls, churches and football and cricket clubs. It's probably no accident that most of the world's great sports have effectively been invented and codified in England. Guilds and liveries have been essential parts of British community life for centuries. Four million Britons are members of the National Trust and over a million are members of the Royal Society for the Protection of Birds.

The starkest modern statement of this worldview comes from Michael Oakeshott. As Gilmour wrote of him:

The existence of liberty in England [depended] on 'the absence from our society of overwhelming concentrations of power.' All other freedoms depended on this one condition of freedom. Authority is diffused between past, present and future. Power also is dispersed 'among all the multitude of interests and organisations of interest which comprise our society' and it is shared between the administration and the Opposition. Indeed the society is both integrated and made more free by the proliferation of voluntary bodies which is the direct result of freedom of association in this country. It is free because by law no one is allowed unlimited power – 'no leader, faction, party or class, no majority, no government, church corporation, trade or professional organisation or trade union.'

Community organisation isn't, of course, a peculiar thing to One Nation, but it is the only tradition that rejects community being dissolved by the power of the market or the power of the state. It respects the communitarian ethos embodied in other, now-dying traditions.

One Nation also rejects the Benthamite concept that community does not exist. Instead, it regards the community as a foundation stone in the development on individuality. The decline of some of these 'little platoons' in recent years has been of concern to One Nation Conservatives, as it increases the prospect of atomisation. Rebuilding these little platoons must be a priority for today's decision-makers.

Community can't be regarded as a footnote in Conservative thinking. Instead, it must be considered as its very core – especially at a time when profound economic and social change has atomised many communities and produced a weakened and deracinated social structure. The growth of loneliness and the decline of neighbourliness is just one symptom of this. A key goal for Conservatives must be countering this feeling of atomisation and isolation by taking the kind of measures to strengthen communal institutions set out in the concluding chapter.

AN ORGANIC THEORY OF CHANGE

One Nation believes in the organic evolution of the state. It feels that British institutions haven't arisen by accident but stand as testament to a unique, and special, island history. This means, for One Nation, that the case for change must be proven and that it must improve the general welfare or the common good. Change based purely on abstract principles, whether they be communist or Hayekian, are viewed with equal scepticism – not only are they flawed but their universalism fails to understand the organic nature of the British constitution or how change grows like an oak tree within England.

One Nation is not, however, resistant to all change. As Burke put it, 'A state without the means of some change is without the means of its conservation.' Disraeli was also clear about this when he said that he was a conservative to preserve what is good about our constitution and a radical to change what is bad. He took this further when he said:

> In a progressive country change is constant; and the great question is, not whether you should resist change which is inevitable, but whether that change should be carried out in deference to the manners, the customs, the laws, the traditions of the people, or in deference to abstract principles and arbitrary and general doctrines. The one is a national system; the other … is a philosophic system.

This, in many ways, is the essence of proper conservatism.

This disposition also means that the economic system can be changed or reformed, as it's based upon meeting societal needs, rather than, as liberals would believe, universal and unchangeable laws. It puts One Nation in a strong position to deliver the kind of reform that people voted for and delivering this reform in a way that will strengthen communal feelings and involve communities, rather than imposing reform based on abstract principles.

Again, this founding pillar of One Nation is completely relevant to our present circumstances. One of the causes of the 2016 referendum was that people felt that change had been happening too quickly and that it was happening *to* them, rather than *with* them. Together, an economic and identity liberalism has created a crisis of insecurity in much of modern Britain, through its push for perpetual movement and perpetual change. The development of a renewed One Nation governing philosophy must be one that values security and community as much as it values mobility and change.

THE SUDDEN DEMISE OF ONE NATION

The collapse of One Nation was remarkably sudden and complete for an ideology that had helped define much of the previous century and had, for the most part, been very successful. Although the 1951–64 governments weren't without blemishes (a certain whiff of snobbery, a refusal to budge after the publication of the Wolfenden Report and the catastrophic cultural vandalism of the Beeching Report), they still must go down as among the most successful of the post-war period. They managed to combine historically high growth, low unemployment, peaceful industrial relations and a relative sense of national cohesion.

The same cannot be said of the Tory government that followed in 1970. Indeed, in many ways, Heathism played a crucial role in devaluing and diminishing One Nation. Heath himself was a managerialist, who didn't share much of the eloquence or even romance that accompanies One Nation at its best. His signature policies illustrated this. The abolition of Resale Price Maintenance, the 'cold shower' of the Common Market or the ugly abolition of historic counties (now gradually being reversed), ignored the importance of continuity and the preservation of what people hold dear. He made the cardinal mistake of turning Tory language from that of the organic and the continuous to that of the revolutionary. He promised 'a change so radical, a revolution so quiet and yet so total'. He also failed to tackle issues that would end up destroying his government and was consumed by the fallacious stop-go idea that the government should pursue growth targets and, with it, store up inflationary pressures.

Although 'Heathism' would become a misjudged shorthand, for some, for One Nation Toryism, it was Heath himself who commenced the reduction of the philosophy from central to marginal. Heath also lost his Chancellor, Iain Macleod, to a heart attack in the House of Commons. Macleod was arguably in a better position than anybody else to redefine One Nation for a different age and his loss was a tragedy for both the country and the party. As his biographer, Robert Shepherd, put it:

Macleod's insight that the existence of One Nation is not inevitable is the crucial, defining difference between Macleod's Toryism and the laissez-faire thinking that dominated the Conservative

Party from the mid 1970s. While favouring market forces, Macleod always realised that if allowed to go unchecked they would be deeply corrosive of social cohesion and inimical to one-nation ... It was the reformist Disraeli who appealed to Macleod ... Macleod fought throughout his career against the notion that laissez-faire, nineteenth-century economics offered a sensible guide for government or society in the second half of the twentieth century.

Of course, the Thatcher revolution wasn't as clear cut as its modern-day adherents would have us believe, and we have considered her legacy in much greater detail in the chapter on economic liberalism. Her leadership was much more pluralist than many assume and much of what people now consider Thatcherism was only even considered canonical after her forced retirement from office. In many ways, it set about to restore the balance that Tories treasure and to spread the property rights that Tories feel are a guarantor of freedom.

What is of interest here is how the One Nation strand in conservatism withered away during the 1980s to the point that economic liberalism had achieved a near-total hegemony by the late 1990s and to be 'Conservative' came to be seen as the same as being 'Thatcherite'. As is discussed elsewhere, what was defined as One Nation in the past few decades bears little comparison to the ideas articulated by Disraeli, Macmillan or Churchill.

Following the debates over economic policy in the late 1970s and early 1980s, many in the One Nation strand simply stopped arguing about economics. Instead, many on the Tory 'left' decided that pursuit of European unity was of much more importance than the unity of their own country.

The eclipse of the One Nation wing coincided with a greater dogmatism on behalf of the free-market right. According to such a worldview, markets were always self-correcting, unemployment was apparently often voluntary and any state intervention was to promote a 'dead hand' and to hinder the market. Dogmatic theories spouted out of think tanks, based on the assumptions of the 'economic man' – as far removed from the empiricism of One Nation Conservatism as can be imagined. Laissez-faire in its cartoon dogma form became as economically reductionist as Marxism, reducing complex humanity to the simplicity of 'homo economicus'. For most of the next few decades, as a pragmatic theory became a hardened ideology, there was nobody to make the One Nation case. The battleground within the Tory Party had moved on to Europe and social issues. This led to over a decade in the electoral wilderness as voters abandoned a party that had become wrapped up in its own ideological faith.

The shift from a pragmatic response to specific circumstances into a hard and unbending ideology would see the party punished with its worst election defeat since the time of the Duke of Wellington. The Tories faced their greatest defeats of modern times in the 1997, 2001 and 2005 elections. In each of these elections, they embraced hard-line approaches to economics, with an increasing dedication to purely market-based solutions. The 1997 campaign saw the Tories arguing against the introduction of a national minimum wage, out of a fear that it would interfere with the self-correcting market. The defeat in 2001 was fought on a manifesto of neo-liberal 'purity'. In 2005, the party had a similarly hard-line manifesto, including 'passports' that enabled people to opt out of public services. Again, the British people weren't impressed by right-wing purity and gave Tony Blair another landslide victory, even though the election was several years after the Iraq War and with his personal ratings plumbing the depths. These cold hard electoral truths should serve as a warning to Tories who seek a return to simplistic purity.

One Nation chroniclers would argue that its very essence is its ability to adapt to different circumstances at different times. It was replaced with an unwavering ideology, which was unable to bend to different circumstances. With this diminution of the One Nation idea, the Tory Party has become both weaker and far less the 'national party' that Disraeli envisioned.

CONSERVATIVE 'MODERNISATION': A MISSED OPPORTUNITY?

The eclipse of the One Nation tradition was seen most clearly with the post-2005 Tory modernisation. David Cameron tried to adopt the One Nation mantle, talking about the pre-Thatcher tradition, placing a picture of Harold Macmillan in his study and giving his imprimatur to ideas such as Phillip Blond's 'red Toryism'. However, he remained committed to the economic settlement that had been passed down from the 1980s. The most impressive rethinking of Tory policy happened around education and social policy, where ministers such as Michael Gove emphasised improving education for the poorest in society and there was an important shift in thinking around the north and infrastructure, with George Osborne's Northern Powerhouse being an important development. Equally, Osborne's pursuit of a national living wage and 'full employment' showed that there were at least the beginnings of a shift in thinking on economic matters.

At the heart of Tory 'modernisation', however, was a belief that the Tory product was fundamentally right, but the brand was seen as 'toxic'. This meant that the Conservatives needed to consider how to present themselves in a more compassionate and compelling way, but not to properly reconsider their approach to political economy.

This also flowed from a fundamental misunderstanding of Labour modernisation and, in particular, the important work of Philip Gould. While Tory modernisers focused on the greater professionalism of Labour's brand under Blair, they ignored the root-and-branch political review that had allowed any brand change to be taken seriously. Labour, for example, abandoned their opposition to EU membership, their unilateralism and their opposition to trade union reform as part of Blair's modernisation. There was no such root-and-branch rethinking of Tory policies, with the conviction being that a 'decontaminated brand' would be sufficient to ensure a modernised party. In many ways, the first generation of Tory modernisers failed to make the argument to the party in the country and didn't seek to expand the party's social base – a failure that created problems for the future.

In some ways, the new generation of Tory modernisers were happy to distance themselves from what went before. Cameron's approach to homosexuality, for example, which was to reach its apotheosis with the welcome introduction of equal marriage, was some distance from a Thatcherism that was, at its worst, socially reactionary. He was happy to apologise for egregious errors, such as Section 28, and some of his bravest ministers, notably Michael Gove, also sought to criticise Thatcher for her emasculation of local government. George Osborne and Matthew Hancock also made welcome moves to make clear that the opposition to the national minimum wage in the 1980s and 1990s was a mistake.

Politically, Cameron moved his party to accept the relative social liberalism (in terms of race and sexuality) of modern Britain, but his commitment to economic liberalism meant that his party risked becoming out of step with the times. A commitment to austerity was one thing, but the first phase of modernisation failed to turn this into a governing philosophy and to consider the impact of harsh welfare policies on the poorest in society. Rather than changing perceptions of the Tory Party, in many ways the first wave of modernisation reaffirmed the idea among voters that the party was for 'the interests of the rich'.

Rhetorically, Cameron also sought to distance his party from the 1980s. He warned the Tories against 'banging on about Europe' and also talked enthusiastically about the 'big society', claiming that 'there is such a thing as society, it's just not the same as the state'. This was a less than subtle attempt to distance his party from Thatcher's declaration that 'there is no such thing as society, just individuals and their families'. He also saw that Tories would fail if public suspicion about their attitude towards public services remained and made great play about his support for both the NHS and high-quality state education. Indeed, the important reforms to state education taken on by Michael Gove, following Tony Blair's academy programme, will probably be regarded as Cameron's major political achievement.

As part of his 'big society', he touched upon some of the themes that we considered earlier – a decline in community spirit and neighbourliness. Some of the more thoughtful modernisers, such as Jesse Norman, took this as reviving the Burkean concept of 'little platoons' and intermediate institutions. Cameron even spoke about a 'broken society', although this was used more as a coded attack on the record of the Labour government than an incisive commentary about the breakdown in important social bonds. There was too little real consideration that what was 'broken' about some elements of society – poor social outcomes, higher levels of anti-social behaviour and high levels of welfare claims – might have been a result of the outcomes of a certain model of political economy that remained largely unchallenged. Deindustrialisation and the failure to adequately deal with it had resulted in low levels of both employment and opportunities. High levels of benefits, in particular incapacity benefit, had been seen by successive ministers as a way of reducing politically damaging unemployment figures.

The biggest missed opportunity came with the approach to the banking crisis. By seeking, ultimately successfully, to portray the recession as one caused by government debt, in which Labour had 'crashed the economy', the Conservatives created political dividing lines, while ignoring the really tough questions that the banking crash had provided in relation to the post-1976 model of political economy.

Far from being self-correcting, the model had shown itself to be inherently unstable and had ushered in a devastating impact on the real economy, which would have been considerably worse without government intervention. In sensing the potential to re-shape the debate into one about government overspending, the Tory modernisers moved the debate from being one about a crisis of unregulated capitalism to one about the limits of government. This was, as events have proven, canny politics.

In turn, however, this prevented any real consideration about the limits of markets or a positive role for the state, meaning that the Tory view on political economy after the banking crash was little changed to the view it held before it. It was a missed oppor-tunity to revive the party's governing philosophy for an age in which what had become known as neo-liberalism had been found to be sorely wanting. This led to a situation in which the party was to be known solely for its approach to austerity and the market – there was no coherent governing philosophy that accompanied this wave of modernisation.

The failure to address voters' concerns about the lack of com-passion in modern Conservatism and its approach to public ser-vices meant that the party still struggled to win the kind of ma-jorities won by their predecessors. In failing adequately to move on from 1980s thinking and to define a governing philosophy that stretched beyond the need for austerity, Mr Cameron was storing up problems for his successor.

WHY ONE NATION MATTERS NOW

The Brexit vote was clearly driven by both cultural and economic concerns, with people feeling that the economic system wasn't working for them, but also that cultural change and dislocation was seen as threatening people's way of life. It was also driven by a sense that politics no longer represented, or even cared about, the views and backgrounds of a great bulk of the people. Economic liberals on the right might be able to address some of the cultural concerns, but, as we have seen, the dynamics of the market mitigate against this and they seem disinclined to check their economic liberalism to address valid economic concerns. Equally, the identity liberals of Corbyn's new left don't seem able to consider how to deliver economic growth and are happy to let cultural concerns go unchecked, with utopian arguments for open borders dominating many on this side of the political spectrum. In such an environment, One Nation provides a route to reunite the country, bring hope to left-behind areas and deliver economic dynamism and social justice.

The decline of One Nation as an economic philosophy, and why it matters, became clear with the widening of divides and the inability to define a positive national message that led to the Brexit vote. By 2017, after decades of ignoring One Nation, or treating it as nothing more than a clever rhetorical construct (even Ed Miliband tried to adopt the language in his most successful party conference speech), Britain had become more akin to 'two nations' than at any time for generations. Parts of the country feel completely left out of the social compact that once bound the country together. Indeed, for many, no such social contract exists at all.

In this environment, the dominant centre-right philosophy of recent years, which has emphasised mobility and individualism, has little to add to the problem of a divided country and people who feel shut out from national prosperity. Similarly, an ideology that has little to add about community, continuity or shared bonds is unlikely to heal national wounds that remain clear and open.

This is not to suggest that One Nation is somehow a panacea – indeed, one of its fundamentals is that it does not *believe* in panaceas. But the main tenets of the economic liberalism that have become the guiding philosophy of 'conservatism' over recent decades cannot alone solve the fundamental problems facing the country today. One Nation ideas of national unity and economic pragmatism, on the other hand, do have an important role to play.

These ideas, set out earlier, strike a chord when confronting the problems our country faces today. Laissez-faire had an important role to play in the late 1970s, when the state had become too large, when enterprise was effectively discouraged and the balance of labour–capital relations had tilted heavily in favour of organised labour. Nowadays, though, the country faces none of those issues. Although Conservatives must continue fighting to support the market economy, they must be careful not to be fenced in by libertarian dogma.

The One Nation idea of national unity must be an important one in a country racked by division and doubt. A belief in community and social institutions is an essential part of renewing those community bonds that have been damaged by atomisation over recent decades.

The disruption of the social contract has come from a mix of economic liberalism and social postmodernism or identity liberalism, which has weakened communal links and increased atomisation. As expressed earlier, the social reforms adopted by Tories in the 1860s and 1870s were introduced precisely because Tories, unlike Liberals, saw the need to tame the rawest edges of capitalism and to ensure that a system didn't deliver profits for the few and suffering for the many.

Reform, rather than revolution, was their mantra. Such a situation applies equally today. The One Nation tradition could be a perfect vehicle for ensuring that growth in national wealth is quickened and that this growth is not retained by a privileged few in a small part of the country but also spread throughout the country. While the opponents of One Nation today either venerate the market mechanism to a ludicrous extent (on the libertarian right) or dismiss any of the benefits of the market mechanism (on the Labour left), it is One Nation that seeks to balance the benefits of the market with the need to ensure that these benefits are shared more widely.

As Gilmour set out, the One Nation economic tradition almost emerged as a Hegelian synthesis. The laissez-faire thesis had produced economic gains with horrendous social distress. The Marxian antithesis proposed an abolition of the system with no real proposal to ensure that economic progress continued. The One Nation synthesis was to retain the economic benefits of the market but also utilise the power of government to spread these benefits and to ensure that fruits were shared by all and nobody in the Kingdom lived in poverty. There is a need for a similar resetting today – the phase of economic liberalism produced economic progress, but not enough people were able to share that prosperity. The Corbynite antithesis would remove these gains in an attempt to tackle social concerns that would be doomed to failure. Only a One Nation synthesis can ensure economic and social progress continue together.

One Nation concepts such as balance, distrust of the untrammelled power of both market and state, and the relevance of communal and national bonds have much to recommend them today. Developments of the past few decades may have nudged GDP forward a few percentage points, but they have made many communities profoundly weaker and diminished feelings of national solidarity. Our next national project must be to regain that sense of solidarity – to make one nation where we have, all too often, become two.

HOW ONE NATION CAN REDRAW THE POLITICAL MAP

British politics stands on the cusp of a major realignment. As discussed in the earlier chapter, party loyalties have become looser, particularly in working-class areas, as Labour becomes more of a middle-class party. There has also been a reduction in the proportion of people who strongly identify with political parties. The SNP landslide in 2015 in Scotland shows how rapidly political loyalties can change.

The 2016 referendum had the added impact of further loosening political ties, particularly in the former industrial towns that we have focused on in this book. Many voters lost faith in the political and economic settlement. Some voters stopped voting altogether, others continued voting Labour out of habit, rather than any profound feelings of loyalty. Both the Alternative Vote referendum and the referendum on EU membership, however, showed that bonds between Labour and what was once their core vote had reached breaking point.

There is, however, a clear opening for the kind of politics articulated by One Nation. A belief in the market mechanism as the best way of creating wealth, but also where the state acts as an enabler to help ensure that all can benefit from prosperity, is an idea with considerable popular support. Economic efficiency combined with social justice could be a winning combination.

By contrast, doubling down on pure economic liberalism would be an electoral cul de sac. Just as few people have real sympathy for old-style socialism, they also have little sympathy for libertarian-style ideas, despite such ideas having widespread support in the media.

A number of commentators on the right have argued that the Tory Party should 'make the case for capitalism' more forcefully. This is an oversimplification of a complex issue. It is one thing to argue that the free market is the best way to create wealth and prosperity – that is something that all Conservatives agree with. It is quite another to mindlessly defend a system, warts and all, when it is patently not delivering the goods for fellow citizens. Rather than engage in posturing, it is best to consider how an economic system can be reformed so that it delivers benefits for everybody, before people start questioning the system itself. There's no point lecturing somebody about 'economic freedom' when that freedom results in long hours of insecure drudgery with limited time to spend with family or friends. The case for capitalism will be made by ensuring that the system actually delivers for those at the lowest end of the income spectrum.

Theresa May's premiership was at its most successful when she promised to tackle the 'burning injustices' in British society and used her conference speech to reject the simplistic nostrums of both socialism and libertarianism. At this stage, her poll ratings reached heights not seen for a Tory leader for decades.

The end result showed that, although many people had flirted with voting Conservative, they had backed away at the last minute. The campaign focused on more conventional Tory messages and there was no mention of the highly popular messaging that the economy and politics should be run in the interests of the many 'not just the privileged few'. The horse race of Brexit and staid messages such as 'strong and stable' dominated and sucked energy from the earlier desire to be seen as the party willing to deliver change to the economic and political settlement. During the over-long campaign, the Tories dialled down the messaging that had made people consider voting Tory for the first time and amplified the messaging that reaffirmed people's previous doubts.

People's reticence to vote Tory isn't because they aren't seen as economically right-wing enough. In contrast, polling makes clear that Conservatives are handicapped by a perceived lack of compassion and by a perception that they are the party of the rich. Voters in some northern and Midlands seats might have sympathy with the Conservatives on issues like Brexit and immigration, but still aren't convinced that they have their economic interests at heart.

Polling by Lord Ashcroft shows that the Conservatives still have to take major steps to shake off their popular image as the party of the rich. It showed that only 22 per cent of voters thought that the Tory Party 'cared about people like me' and only 23 per cent agreed that the party 'wants to help ordinary people get on in life'. Damningly, only 19 per cent of voters felt that the party 'cares about the whole country, not just some types of people', only 20 per cent felt that the it 'stood for fairness' and only 21 per cent agreed that it stood for 'opportunity for all'.

Conservatives didn't make the kind of breakthroughs they hoped for in 2017, although once rock-solid Labour seats like Mansfield and Middlesbrough did move into the blue column. The preceding local elections also saw Conservative gains in once highly unlikely places. This shows that the Tory Party is pushing at the door of realigning politics and redrawing the political map.

To do this, however, they will need to understand why so many voters in the north and Midlands had second thoughts about voting Conservative. This means addressing their economic concerns and tackling issues like the fallout from deindustrialisation and the 'party of the rich' perception. A One Nation agenda would make quite clear that the Tories were on the side of working people in all parts of the country.

Central to this is, of course, building a winning coalition of voters, including the working-class voters in the Midlands and the north who have been let down by generations of politicians and have lost all ties with and faith in the Labour Party. But middle-class voters in the south will also be part of this coalition. Many of these people deserted the Tories last time because of an excessive concentration on Brexit and a perceived lack of compassion. A transformative One Nation agenda would tackle these perceptions head on, and it's reassuring that Boris Johnson has indicated a real willingness to embrace and push such an agenda.

The alternatives to a bold One Nation settlement are two-fold. The first is a managerialist offer, based on an appeal to economic competence and a belief that voters will never elect a Labour Party that has drifted as far to the left as this one. This is a reasonable approach for short-term electoral gain. It does not, however, drive the attitude shift or coalition building that a bold One Nation agenda would. The second alternative is for the party to leave the fairway and veer off to the libertarian rough. There is little evidence that there's any appetite among the public for such a move. Whereas a One Nation agenda could see the party build a bold and broad coalition, an agenda of the libertarian right would have little popular appeal.

The Tories must put forward a vision to show that they can deliver the change to the economic and political settlement that so many voters are demanding. Boris Johnson has made clear that he supports One Nation and backs policies such as higher infrastructure spending, transforming forgotten towns and a higher living wage. By drawing on the traditions of One Nation, Conservatives could transform electoral politics in the UK to their advantage. If they turn their back on One Nation for the sake of ideological purity, however, they risk opening the door to other parties hoping to benefit from the greater fluidity in voting habits.

CHAPTER NINE

TAKING BACK CONTROL: A ONE NATION APPROACH TO REVIVING BRITAIN AND EMPOWERING COMMUNITIES

The rejection of the prevailing economic settlement by so many voters in 2016 cannot simply be wished away by politicians. Voters made it quite clear that they didn't want more vigorous defence of the dogmas that helped create this settlement in the first place. The British people demand fundamental changes to the way in which the economy and politics works. This desire cannot be responded to with more of the same. As Beveridge said upon writing his report, 'a revolutionary moment ... is a time for revolutions, not for patching'.

Rather than more of the same, the country needs a bold and ambitious series of political and economic reforms designed to renew One Nation. This programme of national renewal will have the central aim of empowering people who have long felt a loss of agency to genuinely 'take back control'. The measures that I propose will help tackle the profound economic insecurity felt by many in society, as well as the cultural uncertainty that impacts many of England's towns. This is a manifesto for renewal of long-forgotten towns that falls into several areas:

- Delivering Brexit and using Brexit as a moment of national renewal.
- A programme of national reconstruction, delivering world-class infrastructure for our forgotten towns.
- A sustained programme of devolution which empowers neighbourhoods and communities.
- The creation of prosperity hubs to renew post-industrial towns as engines of low-tax, high-investment innovation.
- The reindustrialisation of forgotten towns.
- Education reform at all levels, including a revolution in vocational education.
- A national housebuilding programme.
- A modern workers' charter, emphasising workers' rights, workplace engagement and employee equity.
- Tax cuts to benefit working people.
- A pay rise for workers.

'Taking back control' was so powerful as a slogan during the referendum campaign because it spoke to a feeling of people's loss of power over their own lives and over the destiny of the country. For decades, people felt that change was something that was done *to* them and that they had no real control over this. This was a message accentuated by a trend towards economic and social liberalism, which has had the impact of perpetuating atomisation, uncertainty and insecurity.

'Taking back control' must be more than a tightly focus-grouped slogan and, instead, should be seen as a mission to re-empower people and communities who have felt cut off from economic success and political discourse for decades. Those 'little platoons' that Burke spoke of should be dramatically re-empowered.

This book started with a consideration of the impact that the politics and economics of the past few decades has had on Consett and places like it. The test for any political programme is whether it benefits people in towns such as these as much as it will benefit people in the City of London or in the prosperous Home Counties.

Fundamentally, this revision to how the economy and politics work should ensure that all citizens feel a sense of agency and empowerment. Citizens who have felt at the periphery of political decision-making and economic prosperity should feel at the centre of both. The goal of this new national project should be to overcome the bitterness and division that has been at the core of national life in recent years and replace it with a sense of unity of purpose around a great national project.

Rebuilding community must be a key priority of the next generation of political leaders. Older community institutions that have fractured cannot simply be rebuilt, nor can a sense of belonging be imposed from the top down, but government can be in a position to empower communities, families and other intermediate institutions.

MAINTAINING PROGRESS

It cannot be overstated that in many ways Britain is a much more pleasant place to live now than it ever has been. LGBT people, women and ethnic minorities are freer from the kind of discrimination and prejudice that was commonplace only decades ago. Women have rights to equal pay and equal treatment and are often the most successful leaders in business and politics. They also have the right to decide what to do with their own bodies regarding reproductive rights. LGBT people can now be open about their love, can marry, adopt and raise children. The kind of racism that was heard on primetime television as recently as the 1980s would be unacceptable now even in a public house.

That is not to say that there isn't more work to be done. Gay people and ethnic minorities still face prejudice. Women are still badly unrepresented in the workplace and the recent government-inspired survey around the gender pay gap says that equal pay is in many ways more rhetoric than reality.

In many ways, though, the country is a better, more tolerant place to live than it was a few decades ago. Few would yearn for a return to the birch and capital punishment and people are right to celebrate the social advances that have been made in recent years. Indeed, in many areas, such as equal marriage, the UK has been one of the leaders in the Western world and should be proud of that. We have already made great progress in the preservation of our precious natural environment. UK emissions were 43 per cent below 1990 levels in 2017 and our beaches are no longer blighted by dirt and pollution. Not many would argue that we should return to a time when British Telecom was the only supplier of telephones and any new phone needed a notice period of several weeks. A return to a time of cripplingly high personal taxation, when the state was over powerful and squeezed out enterprise, is not a glorious past that we should be yearning for.

It's important, however, to consider this progress and ask why so many people don't feel that the country is a better place than it was twenty or thirty years ago. It isn't because they are misty-eyed nostalgics or bigots or feel that their country has been taken from them. Instead, it is because many people have had a sense of certainty and dignity removed from their lives. They feel almost excluded from the body politic and believe that the economic system is run in the interests of people other than them.

Harnessing the great social and economic advances of recent decades, but also being able to extend economic advances to the bulk of the people, should be an important goal for the years ahead. As I've set out, the One Nation tradition, with its emphasis on community, unity, balance and effective use of the state, is, of all the political traditions, best placed to deal with a crisis emerging from an excess of liberalism combined with over-centralisation.

Any political programme needs to be patriotic. To paraphrase Lord Hugh Cecil, loving one's country should also mean wanting to make one's country lovely. It also needs to be populist, but in the best tradition of that term, rather than its debased modern equivalent. As William Jennings Bryan made clear, populism means that the country should be run with the benefit of the majority of the population in mind, rather than a small minority. The common good should be at the core of a renewed politics.

A spirit of vision and positivity should replace the spirit of re-crimination and rancour that has dominated our discourse since 2016. The goal should be simple: to ensure that all citizens feel that they are active parts of the body politic and that they feel the economy is working in their best interest.

TRUSTING THE PEOPLE: CREATING EMPOWERMENT AND AGENCY

There is an important role for the state in creating economic em-powerment, which is based on the enduring principles of One Nation. The role for the state should not, however, be a stultifying or bureaucratic one. In all ways, the goal of the state should be to empower citizens and work to boost entrepreneurship and the private sector across the country. That means the state playing a more active (and empowering) role in some areas and a less active one in others.

The state has an essential part to play in those areas that have been 'left behind'. The market on its own has failed to deliver for these areas and, contrary to economic thinking for much of the past century, hasn't simply rebalanced itself or moved to where 'resources' are less expensive. Indeed, the pattern of recent decades is that sources of growth have become more concentrated, as have sources of deprivation. The state is the only actor that can provide the basis for a growth in empowerment and entrepreneurialism in areas that have long lacked both.

Although the state needs to play a more important and stra-tegic role in the economic space, it also needs to reconsider its role when the actions do anything but empower. While the state has retreated from economic life, it has advanced relentlessly on public health issues, leading to a rise in what many have termed a 'nanny state'.

This is effectively middle-class officials using the law to enforce their lifestyle decisions on working-class people. It's utterly disempowering and represents a new and patronising form of paternalism, which argues that working-class people aren't able to make decisions for themselves and need lifestyle guidance enforced by the state.

As Christopher Snowden has shown in his book *Killjoys*, a relentless stream of guidance and increasingly moralistic public health warnings – about sugar, alcohol consumption and junk food – has led to self-reinforcing and often duplicitous messaging. For example, Public Health England argues that children have, on average, eaten their annual allocation of sugar by June each year. This is then used to argue that sugar consumption is rising. Instead, sugar consumption is actually falling, but PHE's decision to halve their own sugar guidelines in 2015 has allowed them to talk about an epidemic that doesn't exist. Similarly, their self-reinforcing decisions around alcohol and obesity are based around PHE moving the goalposts. Recently, PHE have also pushed for measures to cap the amount of calories in individual foodstuffs and to enforce this by law.

This is the very opposite of empowerment and trusting the people. The idea that people don't know that burgers are bad for you if eaten daily unless they are reminded by a Whitehall finger-wagger is a perverse and wrong-headed one. Even more perverse is the concept that this needs legal intervention and a steady stream of scare stories. The state needs to help empower people in the economic sphere, but it must also rethink its role in wrong-headed lecturing on public health issues.

DELIVERING BREXIT AND USING BREXIT AS A MOMENT OF NATIONAL RENEWAL

Since June 2016, politicians on both sides of the Brexit divide have spent most of their time simply repeating and reframing arguments that dominated that campaign. Too much attention has been placed on what Brexit means for the Westminster village and too little on what it means for the towns and villages around England who actually voted for it.

Politicians and social media activists have continued to seek to define British politics as a never-ending replay of the referendum campaign. Too few politicians or commentators (equally obsessed with the Brexit horse race) have asked the question 'Brexit for what?' It is time to move on from the debate over EU membership, which we were promised that the referendum would 'settle', and, instead, consider how Brexit can be used as a moment of national renewal, with more thought being given to the kind of country that we want to be. As I've argued, this will involve a new political and economic settlement that benefits the majority in the country. *If politicians, and particularly the Conservative Party, fail to deliver Brexit, that will produce a catastrophe of broken trust between government and the governed. Delivering Brexit is a fundamental part of the reforms outlined in this book.*

This means that people across politics need to stop thinking of EU membership as a panacea. Many on the right long regarded the EU as a way to institutionalise market norms. Conversely, the left started to look to Brussels following the crisis of confidence it faced after successive defeats at the hands of Mrs Thatcher. Many substituted a belief in Brussels for a proper programme of economic reform (possibly a reason for New Labour's economic changes being more piecemeal than programmatic). Instead of seeing EU membership as a panacea, politicians have to put the debate on EU membership behind them and place a relentless focus on delivering a new domestic economic and political settlement.

In many ways, Brexit provides an opportunity to develop this new settlement in a way that best suits British towns and that can be democratically responsive. Every EU treaty from the Treaty of Rome onwards has entrenched market liberalism as the raison d'être of the Union. The 'four freedoms' are fundamentally market liberal in tone and philosophy and the European Commission's defining mission has been to defend them. This has been further entrenched through single market rules. The growth and stability pact and its further tightening following the Greek crisis all but eliminated the ability of nation states to utilise Keynesian economic policy within the Eurozone.

Many measures to reform corporate governance or institute an aggressive regional policy would fall foul of EU rules. Any move to give preference to businesses from a particular area would be extremely difficult under EU state aid and non-preference rules. The limits of EU rules may not be as great as some suggest, but they do exist, and they constitute real limitations on the British government to deliver lasting change.

Brexit now offers an opportunity for us to consider what kind of country we want to be and to do this without the limitations of EU rules. It enables us to have a national conversation about what it was that created the belief among so many British citizens that they had been 'left behind' to such an extent that they were willing to ignore the warnings of the entire political, business and entertainment establishment. And it enables us to have a conversation about what we can do to reunite Britain and ensure citizens no longer feel politically and economically abandoned. Even vociferously anti-Brexit campaigners should at least acknowledge that it provides us the freedom to transform our political economy that wouldn't exist if we had remained in the EU.

THE NATION STATE MUST REMAIN THE KEY VEHICLE FOR REFORM

There has been a mistaken assumption on both left and right in recent decades that the combined forces of identity liberalism and economic liberalism would produce an 'open' environment in which borders became increasingly meaningless, national cultures became amorphous and fluid, and nation states became relatively powerless. Cultural liberals, with a belief in open borders, formed a slightly unholy alliance with economic liberals who endorsed the benefits of footloose capital. Both camps saw the nation state as gradually being weakened and enfeebled by larger, dominant economic and cultural forces, with transnational bodies effectively acting as regional and global arbiters. The argument was that the nation state was a nineteenth-century institution that wasn't suitable for the needs and demands of the twenty-first century.

Recent history has been unkind to such a utopian worldview. And rightly so. It has only ever been pushed by a small minority of the population (although a much larger proportion of elites) and has utterly failed to understand, as many utopian ideas have previously failed to understand, the importance of human nature.

The truth remains that for democracy to be a success it must be based around communities of mutual understanding and respect, bound by common culture, language, history and understanding. Only the nation state has sufficient commonalities of interest and culture to make democracy legitimate, as well as providing a large enough governance area to make democracy workable and effective.

It's clear that, despite the claims of a small but powerful minority, most people regard the main source of legitimate representation as being at a national, not transnational, level (witness the declining turnout for the European Parliament elections, which has gone down from 63 per cent to 50 per cent across the EU despite the powers of the Parliament relentlessly increasing).

Only through national democracy do people feel that they have a sense of agency and control against impersonal forces. Recent years should have persuaded people that the national remains the pivotal political sphere and that transnational or global ideas have no emotional base. The Brexit vote was only the most high-profile protest against a governance arrangement that put transnational technocracy over national democracy, where people knew that their opinions and votes could be reflected by accountable politicians.

As such, any programme of economic and political renewal must be based around the nation state and the smaller communities within that nation state. It should be about reviving democratic, accountable institutions, but also ensuring that the nation state has the economic power to be able to transform the lives of all citizens. A programme of economic rearmament must include a real focus on previously 'left-behind' areas and ensure that British young people have the skills necessary to succeed in an emerging economy.

A PROGRAMME OF NATIONAL RECONSTRUCTION, DELIVERING WORLD-CLASS INFRASTRUCTURE FOR OUR FORGOTTEN TOWNS

A central theme of this book has been that towns and villages across the country have been ignored for too long. They have seen little real benefit from the substantial economic changes over recent decades and no longer feel that political parties adequately represent or articulate their best interests. Low-skill, low-pay jobs predominate, often accompanied by low levels of job security and diminishing opportunities to spend time with friends and family.

All too often, town centres have lost their vibrancy, dominated by shops that either are empty or sell cut-price bargains, holidays or betting opportunities. These towns were once mono-industrial, and the type of work that has replaced manufacturing hasn't been adequate in terms of stature or working conditions. Housing stock is often old and dilapidated, with design of housing estates lacking creativity and communal spaces. Bright young people tend to leave the towns to attend university and then work in large cities, predominantly in London, creating a brain drain that accentuates divisions and decline. This has resulted in what some academics have described as 'urban shrinkage', where some towns and cities face both a falling population and rapidly diminishing new business growth. This has been felt in both post-industrial towns and coastal communities, which have the commonality of failing to replace old industries with new ones.

Most of these towns lost interest in politics years ago but still tended to return Labour MPs with sizeable majorities. This lack of competitive politics meant that party machines could ignore these seats in favour of more competitive 'marginal' constituencies. That is shorthand for scores and scores of towns and villages across the country, and it's a level of decline that can't be allowed to continue for much longer.

There must be a concerted and bold programme of national reconstruction, with the aim of turning around decades old decline. This requires a level of infrastructure spending not seen since shortly after the Second World War, with the goal of ensuring that those communities that have often come last in the thoughts of decision-makers can now boast the best infrastructure in the Western world.

The goal of this isn't to expand the state. Instead, the goal is to boost the private sector and entrepreneurship across the country. Only substantial investment in the right kind of infrastructure by the government will provide the foundation stone for a vibrant private sector in parts of the country where it doesn't exist at the moment. Only proper investment in road, rail and light rail into all town centres will provide the basis for towns and the private sector within them to thrive.

Some would argue that this would entail reckless spending at a time when the UK economy is still emerging from a substantial structural deficit. They would, however, be mistaken. Infrastructure investment is like sowing the seeds for a great tree – the tree itself is impossible without the seeds. Moreover, as set out earlier, the fact that difficult decisions were made to cut the deficit several years ago means that a programme of infrastructure spending is now justifiable and possible. Because of the measures to tackle the unsustainable deficit, the cheapness of debt now means that spending for investment can be substantially increased.

Without adequate infrastructure, parts of the UK are doomed to fall further behind economically and socially. For too long, people in some parts of the country have had to put up with poor or non-existent train services, slow and lumbering broadband connections, indifferent roads and cutbacks in bus services.

The idea that transformation can be driven purely from Whitehall is one that belongs in the past. To paraphrase Douglas Jay, the man in Whitehall really does *not* know best. When decisions have been made in Whitehall, the chief beneficiaries have tended to be London and, in some cases, marginal constituencies needing a reminder of Whitehall love ahead of an election.

To change this situation, infrastructure spending should form the centrepiece of a programme of national reconstruction, with the aim of ensuring road, rail and technology links in long-forgotten places become world-class. This can be funded from the centre but must be directed at a local level, with a national baseline of infrastructure providing the basis for innovation with minimum standards. Boris Johnson's announcement of Crossrail between Manchester and Leeds is a welcome sign that the Prime Minister is quite serious about delivering transformative infrastructure to the north.

A SUSTAINED PROGRAMME OF DEVOLUTION

Devolution in the past few years has been welcome, as has talk of a Northern Powerhouse, but this needs to be redoubled – with substantial powers being given to well-known local figures who are able to champion the interests of the community. At present, mayoral figures are being elected on the promise of campaigning for greater powers. Indeed, Dan Jarvis, the Mayor of South Yorkshire, is retaining his role as Barnsley MP as the mayoral position is unpaid.

Central government should be prepared to provide funding to local and regional authorities in order to provide infrastructure but, within reason, they should devolve powers over this to the local or regional level. There is no reason that decisions over local transport policies should be made in Whitehall – such a mentality leads to the kind of chaos seen by the railways in much of Yorkshire and the north-west over recent years. It also tends to lead to decisions being made that benefit the places where most ministers and civil servants are based.

Similarly, mayors, in towns as well as cities, should be given the powers to raise money themselves, rather than having to depend on the generosity of Whitehall. They should be able to work with local authorities to have proper strategic power over a region, rather than this being decided at a national level. Regional mayors should at least have the powers invested in the Mayor of London and, if possible, the real powers of all mayors, including in London, should be increased. Equally, mayors should be able to push forward the technical education revolution that I call for elsewhere in this chapter.

Devolution, however, shouldn't stop at the mayor's office. It's imperative that proper power should be devolved to the lowest level possible, including to towns and communities. This is particularly important for those 'left-behind' communities, which need inspired and empowered local leadership combined with nationally delivered infrastructure and the right skills for a prosperous future.

EMPOWERING NEIGHBOURHOODS AND COMMUNITIES

Increasing community feeling also means increasing community engagement to tackle local issues, such as cutting anti-social behaviour, improving education and enhancing community facilities. This is with the obvious caveat that many people don't have the time or the inclination to dedicate themselves to making a difference to their community. Others, however, have the inclination, but decades of economic and identity liberalism have robbed them of the time and the ability to carry it through.

The excellent David Brooks has pointed to a number of ways in which neighbourhoods and communities can be empowered and revived. As he put it, the difference between communitarianism and liberalism is summed up by the concept of a swimming pool: libertarians only clean the part you're swimming in. As he argues:

> It could be that the neighborhood, not the individual, is the essential unit of social change ... One of the signature facts of the internet age is that distance is not dead. Place matters as much as ever, and much more than we ever knew ... The typical American adult *lives eighteen miles* from his or her mother. The typical college student enrolls in a college thirteen miles from home. A study of Facebook friends nationwide found that 63 percent of the people we friend live within 100 miles. Americans move less these days, not more ... Work by the economist Raj Chetty and others shows that children who grow up in one neighborhood can have drastically different life outcomes than people who grow up in demographically similar neighborhoods nearby ... The fact is that human behavior happens in contagious, networked ways. Suicide, obesity and decreasing social mobility spread as contagions ... Thinking in neighborhood terms means radical transformation in how change is done ... It means adjusting the structures of the state so that the neighborhood is an important structure of self-government, rather than imposing blanket programs willy-nilly across neighborhood lines.

An organisation called Strive Together in the USA is leading community-based change, and research from Stanford

University suggests that such change is delivering a clear, positive social impact and improving communal success and communal bonds. So-called collective impact projects are largely community-based aimed at tackling defined problems together and are seen as having a positive effect. The more power is devolved to the neighbourhood or community level, the more relationships, as opposed to impersonal data, matter and the more local people feel an urgency and a need to get involved and make things better for their local area. Place matters at least as much in the UK as it does in the US, and the importance of place has been ignored by many politicians for decades.

Closer to home, the 'Wigan Deal' has provided a template for what a community-driven approach might look like in the UK. The town had to respond to cuts of around £160 million in its budget following austerity and, in doing so, it formed a deal with residents: that the council would freeze Council Tax, invest in communities and redesign services, but residents would become more involved in communities. As part of this, the council increased funding for over 450 community-based initiatives. This saw a substantial boost in citizen satisfaction, improvements in health and education outcomes and an enhanced innovation. The example of Wigan, rather like its peers from the USA, is obviously not flawless, but it does show that, with the right approach, local communities can become engaged rather than alienated.

Is this suggesting that the best approach for central government to take is a hands-off one and let local communities get on with it? Partially, yes, but government can also play a much more enabling role than that. For one, it can ensure that communities have the facilities to congregate around. A number of studies have shown that communities with widely used public spaces, such as libraries, community centres and pubs, are important to generating community values. Many of these facilities have been diminished in recent years, resulting in fewer places for communities to come together and help build change at a neighbourhood level. Certainly, in the case of libraries and Sure Start centres, this decline has been driven in part by a reduction in central funding. Rebuilding community infrastructure is something that central government has a responsibility to play a role in. Enhancing community engagement, however, should be the responsibility of local authorities and communities themselves.

Maintaining community spaces isn't just about the high street – although that is, of course, crucially important. It's also about restoring the town centre as a place where members of the community congregate and spend time together. Devolution to local areas needs to provide the space for local areas to innovate, but central government should also facilitate this freedom in a number of ways. First, they should ensure that it's possible to be based in the centre of the town without losing money – there's a reason, after all, why charity shops, who are exempt from business rates, have come to dominate most high streets. It seems reasonable at least, in combination with the prosperity hubs discussed below, to provide support for town centres. The towns with the highest levels of deprivation should be able to charge the lowest level of business rates in order to help rejuvenate their town centres. Second, government should encourage community-based regeneration in an innovative way, with a promise to match a multiple of an amount raised locally for innovative town centre regeneration projects and use of community space.

As Paul Swinney has argued, town and city centres should be at the core of local economies and local society, with a focus on jobs and businesses also being located in the town centre rather than in distant business parks. This, combined with the infrastructure provided in the Programme of National Reconstruction, must be designed to ensure that town centres are well connected by road and rail and have world-class internet connectivity.

PROSPERITY HUBS: RENEWING POST-INDUSTRIAL TOWNS

Devolution alone is not going to solve the issue of towns and areas that have been left behind for decades. A programme that invests to ensure that all towns and villages are properly connected will help enable these places to compete where they previously had both hands tied behind their back because of dereliction of duty by successive governments, leading to sub-standard connectivity. However, left-behind areas will be still be behind and asked to catch up from a standing start.

Local communities need the power to innovate in order to deliver substantial and transformative change. The role of central government is to provide the overlapping transport and digital infrastructure to ensure a *national basic minimum of infrastructure* that is still among the global best. This must be fast and reliable in order to allow businesses to grow and towns to prosper.

But localities, and left-behind localities in particular, should be strongly encouraged and incentivised to innovate. Within reason, there should be as few restrictions on this innovation as possible.

Government should give special powers to elected mayors of the twenty to thirty towns and conurbations that have the worst deprivation and worklessness in the country. They should be declared as priority *prosperity hubs* and provided with extra government resources to update physical, digital and housing infrastructure. Government should also provide them with extra powers, with a mandate to do *whatever it takes* to bring about social, cultural and economic regeneration and the ability, facilitated by government, to work with global experts in business and government around the world who have delivered successful urban renewals elsewhere.

PROSPERITY HUBS AS ENGINES OF LOW-TAX, HIGH-INVESTMENT INNOVATION

They would also be exempted from national rules around taxation and other areas and be able to charge zero business rates. The main area in which they would not be exempted would be the minimum standards of workers' rights set out in the Workers' Charter.

It would be wise to consider global examples of success in urban renewal. They have great infrastructure, as discussed earlier, but Detroit's empty monorail stands as a case study that infrastructure alone will not regenerate a struggling area. Infrastructure needs to be combined with genuine incentives to invest. Austin, Texas, for example, not only has the digital infrastructure that has made it the US capital for tech start-ups; it also has no state corporate or personal taxation. Government should consider ways to allow prosperity hubs to encourage investment by having lower rates of corporate or personal taxation, as well as zero business rates and measures to encourage investment, such as boosting capital allowances nationally and in prosperity hubs in particular.

Local areas would also be encouraged to take steps to ensure that any economic improvement doesn't result in a 'gentrification', which exiles local people from their own town. This includes having good-quality social housing and making sure that local people have the skills needed to prosper in the emerging economy. A land value uplift, which pays a dividend to the local community, could also be considered to ensure that local residents benefit from improved prosperity.

The local authority should utilise the power that comes from land ownership to create public housing, where rents aren't linked to market values, as well as commercial units on the high streets, which can be let out to small businesses and local start-ups at below-market rents.

A clear goal would be to create conurbations that become desirable places to live, work and raise a family. These would also be conurbations that young people not only don't want to leave, but want to return to if they have already left. Good places not only to start a business, but to grow a business. Global evidence shows that most successful places combine economic dynamism with strong cultural and sporting offerings and a real sense of place and identity.

Some might choose to develop substantial tax incentives for businesses to relocate. Others might choose to embark on a cultural regeneration programme. Some might target investment grants at small businesses that embark on scientific or technological research. Others might combine with large companies to have a town-wide drive to be focused around specific skills and industries. Some might choose to be the advance party for the revolution in skills and vocation. Others might use newfound powers to differentiate in terms of drug policy – some towns in North America, for example, have marked themselves out as creative communities through such relaxed laws. In this way, left-behind communities will offer a way ahead for the rest of the country, rather than scurrying for a way to catch up.

This initiative should be run in alliance with the free-port scheme, which allows ports to import and export goods without taxes or tariffs and could also play an important role in revitalising port areas that have been suffering long-term decline.

ENCOURAGING HIGH PRODUCTIVITY INVESTMENT OUTSIDE OF THE SOUTH-EAST

The successful relocation of large parts of the BBC to Salford in Manchester has shown how effective large-scale moves of major employers can be. Not only were jobs created directly by the BBC, but the move also created jobs in supporting sectors and helped to double the size of the creative and digital economy in Greater Manchester. The move of Nissan to Sunderland in the 1980s also created growth in the wider supply chain.

The presence of a large 'anchor' employer plays an important role in encouraging others to move to an area. Government should do two things to provide greater momentum in low-prosperity parts of the country. The first is connected to the creation of prosperity hubs – central government can work with these hubs to develop ways to encourage large employers to base in these hubs. This might mean encouraging large employers presently based in London to relocate.

CUTTING CORPORATION TAX
TO ENCOURAGE INVESTMENT

Inward investment can also play a role in increasing productivity, boosting skills investment and enhancing the 'supply chain' and network effects in a local area. Government can help incentivise this by providing a perfect environment for business investment, particularly in areas that have long been struggling. The experience of Ireland, which now has higher investment in skills and much higher GDP per head than the UK (it has gone from 25 per cent below the UK to 45 per cent above the UK in twenty-seven years) shows that the level of corporation tax can have a real impact on levels of investment. That is why, as O'Brien and others have advocated, we should aim to have a national corporation tax level at least as low as Ireland's and ideally lower. As mentioned earlier, prosperity hubs should also be allowed to consider having corporation tax that is at zero or, at the very least, below the national level in an attempt to rocket-boost local growth and investment. Government should also consider whether it is practical to allow poorly performing regions, such as the north-east and West Midlands, to have rates of corporation tax that are below the national average in order to encourage investment outside of the south-east.

As we'll discuss below, changes to the regime around capital allowances represents an important part of measures to encourage investment in areas that have been struggling. Government should also consider learning from successful examples overseas, such as South Korea (which boasts the highest level of innovation in the world). South Korea has 'investment zones', supported by the government, which provide incentives around tax, purchase of land, renting and capital grant around high-value industries that are considering investing in Korea. Such an approach should also be taken in the prosperity hubs and beyond.

RELOCATING GOVERNMENT DEPARTMENTS

Another mechanism to boost struggling towns is something that government has direct control over: the location of government departments and their agencies. The case has long been made that proximity to ministers means that senior civil service jobs must be based in London. Modern technology has made that argument irrelevant. If modern businesses are able to run successfully with executives based on different continents, there is no reason why modern government should not work effectively with civil servants and ministers based in different cities.

Government should consider significant relocation in order to boost regeneration efforts and to substantially rebalance the economy. Rather than taking a piecemeal approach and relocating government agencies, an ambitious government should consider relocating entire government departments to outside of London. There is little reason that departments such as DCLG, DEFRA, BEIS or DWP, for example, need to be based in the capital. The government should consider moving them outside of London.

The UK would not be the only country to do this. Instead, it would be part of a global trend, with countries as diverse as Mexico, South Korea and Norway all moving significant parts of their civil service machine outside of national capitals. Moving departments out of London won't just boost regional economies and create broader supply chain benefits, it will also serve to change the mindset of senior civil servants and ministers, who are too often submerged in a south-eastern frame of mind.

REINDUSTRIALISING FORGOTTEN TOWNS

One of the many welcome breaks with laissez-faire in recent years has been the revival of the concept of 'industrial strategy', previously written off as pointless interference with the self-regulating market. Most successful Western economies have some form of industrial strategy, which entails cooperation between government, business and workers. Harold Macmillan understood this when he created the National Economic Development Council. Likewise, Michael Heseltine was right to describe the need for an industrial strategy as 'urgent and unavoidable' and that the 'simplistic language of getting off one's back, sacking a few civil servants and undoing red tape is a million light years away from the responsibility of presiding over major technologically advanced programmes on which our industrial wellbeing depends'.

There is clear scope for reindustrialising the British economy

– not to recreate old-style heavy industry but to ensure that parts of the country that have industrial and engineering culture and history can use this to energise a new generation of manufacturing. The share of manufacturing as a proportion of the economy has fallen from 40 per cent in the 1950s, to 33 per cent in 1970, to 17 per cent in 1990 and is at 10 per cent today. This is well below the levels in those countries that have the kind of dual-track vocational system that we will discuss later, such as Germany (23 per cent) and Switzerland (18 per cent), and some way below South Korea (29 per cent), often perceived as the most innovative economy in the world. These countries also have strong investment in research and development, at both governmental and private-sector level. The towns that once depended on manufacturing have a mindset, spirit and enduring skillset to reindustrialise, if provided the right infrastructure, skills and incentives.

Observers such as Mariana Mazzucatto have even pointed out that government research and development has been at least indirectly responsible for most of the innovation that we have seen over recent years, including the iPhone. She argues that government can both make markets and provide the fuel necessary for innovation.

That the concept of an industrial strategy is acceptable again is, of course, hugely welcome. What should concern us now is not whether there should *be* an industrial strategy (that should answer itself), but how it should be *used* to help bolster those communities that have failed to prosper in recent decades. A concern about the present application of the industrial strategy might serve to bolster the areas around Oxford and Cambridge, which are already displaying potential in the artificial intelligence (AI) field, and we must consider ways to broaden the geographical spread of already excellent research.

An industrial strategy needs to be part of a wider programme of reform. As such, all elements in this chapter work together. An industrial strategy needs workers with the right skills, an engaged workforce, decent infrastructure and banks that are willing to invest in longer-term projects outside of the south of England. The long-noted problems that an industrial strategy needs to solve currently remain for all to see: as an economy we don't invest enough, aren't long-term enough and the economy isn't productive enough.

Negativity about the nature of politics and economics shouldn't blind us to the fact that the UK has a huge number of strengths, and these strengths should be built upon and shared more widely. This country, for example, leads the world in AI and the mobile internet economy – two elements that we know will be fundamental in economic success or failure in the future.

And many of our existing strengths lie close to those areas that feel left behind (because they have been). Sunderland, for example, boasts the most productive car plant in Europe and one that, as noted earlier, could be a model of employer–employee cooperation. Universities in Newcastle, Durham and Manchester lead the world in various research fields. Sunderland University is a world leader in computer game development. One of the challenges we face is harnessing these strengths, while also undertaking more fundamental reform.

REINDUSTRIALISATION THROUGH ENCOURAGING INDUSTRIAL INVESTMENT AND IMPROVING ACCESS TO CAPITAL

Industrial strategy should involve encouraging universities to work actively in their local areas to ensure that their research is actively applied in their local area. Government should also co-sponsor *National Centres of Applied Research*, which will engage universities and local employers in specific research areas. These National Centres should be based within the prosperity hubs.

Part of an industrial strategy should involve government providing seed investment, particularly in businesses investing in left-behind areas. It should also aim to increase the level of R&D investment from both government and the private sector to well above the OECD average. The government has already, laudably, sought to increase this through its industrial strategy. It should, however, aim to go further by using tax incentives to encourage further R&D spend and using the National Centres of Applied Research to drive innovation.

As well as introducing these National Centres of Applied Research, government should also reform the system around capital investment, so businesses are no longer disincentivised from investing in R&D and skills. A study by Oxford University has shown that the UK has the least generous tax allowances in the whole of the G20. It can't be coincidental that the UK also has the lowest level of investment in the G20 and has done for many years. This has also worsened the level of deindustrialisation in the UK. All of this has particularly hit the towns that we have discussed in this book. Capital allowances for investment, whereby investment is deducted from corporation tax, should be enhanced so they are the most generous in the G20. We should also go further in the prosperity hubs and potentially also in entire regions, with even more generous allowances being used in these areas.

Sam Bowman makes a convincing case that we should go even further in using the capital allowances system to encourage investment. This is through something called 'full expensing', which allows businesses to deduct the value of the investment immediately from their corporation tax, rather than removing it incrementally over the lifetime of the investment. A number of studies show that 'full expensing' can make a dramatic difference to the levels of investment. A study looked at the impact of full expensing. When it was introduced in various US states, it increased investment by almost 18 per cent, production output by over 10 per cent and wages by 2.5 per cent. Similar double-digit rates of investment growth have been seen in other studies. Full expensing of capital allowances is a reform that should be rolled out nationwide in due course, but it should be first rolled out in the prosperity hubs and in regions that have lower than average GDP per head.

REINDUSTRIALISATION THROUGH IMPROVED ACCESS TO FINANCE

Towns outside of the south-east are going to continue to struggle if they keep hitting brick walls when it comes to access to capital. Most banks are located within the south-east and contain cultural bias. Moreover, banks undoubtedly feel that large-scale investment in a low-growth town with minimal transport links is much less attractive than the same level of investment in a vibrant city.

There is a crucial role for government in correcting this imbalance. One of the reasons that many European countries, such as Germany with its Kreditanstalt für Wiederaufbau, have a more 'balanced' economy is that they have financial institutions based outside of the financial capital, with local interests at heart.

The 2008 banking crash made clear that the UK's financial system was in urgent need of reform, but it remains overleveraged, deeply geographically concentrated, unreformed and unwilling to lend to businesses outside of the south-east. The decline of building societies also meant a decline of locally based institutions with a direct stake in the local economy.

This model of regional and local investment banks must be utilised in the UK. These banks would be based at a regional level, with a strong local identity and a remit to invest in productive business. These could well be funded by existing high street, or investment, banks who would be incentivised to provide initial start-up capital.

A successful local or regional bank would be based on successful relationships with local business, rather than the automated, centralised and detached model that dominates banking in the UK today. Instead, local and regional banks would have a direct interest in building the local and regional economy. Government might also consider tying consumer lending to the level of lending to business, which would incentivise existing high street banks to play their part in increasing investment in British business.

Government policies can also help support home-grown R&D and industry in a number of ways. The UK can no longer be seen as 'easy game' when it comes to takeovers, particularly when this results in a diminution of the research and development base in the UK. This is in contrast to inward investment by foreign firms, which boosts R&D and skill spend. A public interest test regarding takeovers is long overdue. Equally, government can use its procurement policy to help jet-propel British industry. It is a nonsense that so many government contracts are awarded to overseas companies when British businesses are able to provide the same level of service. It is only right that government at all levels should introduce a 'buy British' preference within their procurement rules.

EDUCATION REFORM AT ALL LEVELS, INCLUDING A REVOLUTION IN VOCATIONAL EDUCATION

In the UK, we are rightly proud of having so many great academic institutions. Our universities more than hold their own in the global league tables for academic and research excellence, in a way that institutions from other European countries fail to do. The goal for the next few decades is to replicate that success in the vocational field and to ensure that pursuing an education doesn't have to entail leaving one's home town. Attending university should not be the norm, and those who do choose to go should not necessarily have to leave their home town either.

As I've set out throughout this book, the UK economy is at risk of becoming a low-skill, low-wage, low-productivity economy. An obsession with academic education is leaving us with skills we don't need and encouraging brain drains from town centres. It is also leaving our economy short of the skills we do need and our forgotten towns short of the young people necessary to help rebuild them.

A bold and revolutionary change to the way in which we view education is essential. This would be headed by the introduction of world-class vocational colleges, backed by employers, unions and employer organisations.

THE BEST TEACHERS IN THE AREAS OF GREATEST NEED

If we are serious about narrowing the economic and social divide, the first imperative must be ensuring that the poorest areas have high-quality early years education, plus the best schools and the most inspiring teachers. The education reforms of both the Blair and, particularly, the Cameron governments stand as among the greatest achievements of those administrations. The 'London Challenge' provides a brilliant example of how schools in an entire city can turn their performance around. The focus now, though, has to be placed on improving those schools in the poorest post-industrial areas.

Government should provide additional funding to encourage the best teachers to relocate to schools in the poorest towns. It would also encourage school leaders, with a track record of success in other schools (including in the private sector), to lead both existing and new schools in left-behind towns. Good practice would also be shared as part of a 'Prosperity Hub Challenge', with the goal of having the highest standards of educational achievement in post-industrial towns within ten years. Allied to this will be a task force dedicated to increasing the educational performance of boys in these towns in particular.

A DUAL-TRACK VOCATIONAL REVOLUTION
IN SCHOOL AND AFTER SCHOOL

A revolution in schooling should be accompanied by a vocational revolution, taking in post-school years. For years, British politicians have tipped their hat towards the strong vocational systems in Switzerland, Germany, Austria, Denmark and Norway, where between 30 and 70 per cent of young people participate in some form of vocational education. But British politicians have failed to raise the credibility of vocational education so that it matches that of academia. Middle-class people who complain about too many people going to university would still generally blanch at the idea of their own children pursuing a vocational course.

The clear divide between the academic and the vocational has had the effect of hollowing out towns, marking a clear social divide between graduates and the rest. Universities have tended to benefit financially from the pursuit of increased tuition fees by successive governments, but vocational and further education colleges have endured frequent funding cuts.

In the northern European states with strong vocational systems, the vocational is clearly seen as on a par with the academic. In many ways, such as delivering personal growth in a lasting career and delivering workplace experience at an early stage, it is seen as superior to an academic education. In these countries, there are also clear routes between academic and vocational train-ing – choosing one does not mean ignoring the other. Vocational education is also a clear part of the cultural bloodstream, with strong support from business, unions, employer groups and communities.

The advantages of a strong, well-respected vocational stream are felt throughout society. This is seen nowhere more clearly than in Switzerland and Germany, both of which have a more balanced, less concentrated economy and strong manufacturing sector. In these examples of a so-called dual system, young people decide on a vocational or academic route before they turn sixteen, but also maintain an academic track with the vocational route. Careers that would be associated with graduates in the UK, such as finance, computer programming or engineering, are deeply as-sociated with the vocational track, emphasising the importance of employer cooperation in making such a system work.

A vocational system also reflects the kind of skills that are in growing demand from employers, such as experience and soft skills. Employers globally have also shown an increasing demand for 'tertiary-additional' education. Put simply, the UK system as it stands does not deliver any of these things, whereas students in Switzerland and Germany earn skills and experience in actual work settings, increasing their usefulness to employers and the economy as a whole. Experience from Switzerland shows that private companies who participate in the dual-learning system are enthusiastic about it and benefit from it, meaning that, as well as gaining skilled workers, there is also a wider business model for participation. This is partially because of state support for the system and the fact that there is a 'third learning location', where young people learn additional skills that will be applicable to the workplace. That is a part of the model that must be replicated in the UK.

There are, of course, important social and cultural reasons for the success of the dual model in places like Switzerland and Germany. They cannot be transplanted lock, stock and barrel to a different economy and a different culture such as the UK. Nevertheless, a move to a more defined vocational model will mark an important change in the UK economy and a crucial shift in many of England's forgotten towns. It will also mean that education in these towns will be focused on providing satisfying growth to young people and will ensure that towns have ready access to the skills needed to thrive in today's economy and the high-skill economy of the future. It is also important to note that many of the post-industrial towns have a strong historical culture linked to apprenticeship, skill and vocation, so the development of a strong vocational offering is entirely consistent with this culture.

Such reforms will not come easily. They will need to sit alongside cultural and economic reforms that shift the economic model to focus on skill, worker engagement and inclusive growth. They would encourage strong local economies and an increased focus on skills and business, embedding local employers in a culture in a way that has now been lost but was once embodied by the Shotley Bridge swordmakers. Whereas some present 'apprenticeship schemes' don't provide a fully rounded educational experience, these proposals would produce a young population with the skills necessary both to prosper and to help revive their communities.

DEVELOPING GREAT VOCATIONAL INSTITUTIONS
IN PARTNERSHIP WITH BUSINESS

The kind of reforms proposed would not have the goal of weakening our great academic institutions, merely supplementing them with great vocational institutions. Partially modelled on the 'third learning location' in many northern European countries, they should also be explicitly built on engagement with major local and national employers, making it clear that the new vocational network is deeply linked to strong career development. This would also need a shift in employers' sole reliance on universities to provide education and training.

These new institutions would be developed with government and private sector investment, providing general skills-based training and a focus on the skills that that employer is famous for. For example, government and local authorities could work with Nissan in Sunderland to develop a Nissan Academy for Advanced Engineering. Banks could give a little back by sponsoring accountancy academies. Global tech firms could sponsor academies for AI and computer programming.

These vocational colleges would obviously not be the sole route of employees for these key companies, but they would provide a source that currently doesn't exist. Young people would be able to choose between the vocational or educational route at the age of fourteen. If they choose the former, they would sign on to schemes designed and run by employers and employer organisations. Students would spend time in the workplace and in these academies, learning both work-related skills and core academic courses, notably maths and English.

At no point would further academic studies be ruled out, and these central courses should be a core part of any vocational course. As in the Swiss example, in particular, there should be clear routes between academic and vocational tracks, and employers should lead the way in ensuring a parity of esteem between the two.

As discussed, at present, the UK is below the European median for amount invested in employee training. As David Goodhart has identified, the open-door immigration policy of recent years has meant that employers have had no incentive to invest in British talent when they could just as easily employ people who already have the requisite skills. A post-Brexit environment makes this much more difficult for employers, so there is a need for them to consider skills more seriously, as well as a deeper social obligation to do so. With this in mind, the UK should have a target of being over the European average for investment in employee training within five years and in the top three within ten. This revolution in education would be a key element in attempts to reindustrialise long-forgotten parts of the country.

Investing properly in technical and vocational education isn't just important for young people; it also matters for the wider economy and can play a central role in reskilling and lifelong learning. This is another reason that vocational institutions should have a key role in the design of a vocational system. These should be engaged with government and employers in ensuring that existing workers have the skills necessary to prosper in the changing world – making lifelong learning a reality, rather than a buzzword. This could be done in tandem with the idea of national learning accounts, which have been promoted by a number of commentators, and allow workers to engage in training through-out their career.

Such a change isn't going to happen overnight. In the interim, more work must be done to ensure that existing vocational offers are able to grow in esteem. As thoughtful Tory moderniser Rob Halfon has argued, degree apprenticeships offer an important way of continuing education while gaining real-world experience, and they should be 'rocket-boosted'.

A NATIONAL HOUSEBUILDING PROGRAMME

BUILDING SO WE HAVE THE HOUSES WE NEED

As we have seen, the housing crisis that has been impacting the UK for over a decade has bitten in northern towns as well as southern cities. Those who are on low pay all too often find themselves trapped in poor-quality private rented accommodation – working longer hours, but seeing more and more of their pay swallowed down a dark hole of rent expenses. While homeownership has fallen by over 7 per cent since its peak in 2003, the level of private renting has more than doubled.

Homeownership should continue to be championed – it increases a sense of belonging, gives people a stake in the economy and enhances communities. The state should use its power to build more houses and ensure that people at all levels of the income scale are able to buy them. The property-owning democracy is as noble an aspiration now as it was when Noel Skelton first coined the term.

It is clear that the private sector is either unable or unwilling to build sufficient houses to meet the ambition of such a property-owning democracy. It's equally clear that government must have a role in building houses, otherwise any supply side scheme designed to boost homeownership will merely lead to inflated house prices and bloated developers. We need a national house-building programme driven by government.

The first step in this is pushing forward a scheme that will lead to a new generation of low-rent homes, with a fast track to homeownership. These would be genuinely affordable, with rent no higher than a third of the salary of the take-home pay for a worker on a low income. These new, low-rent homes could be funded directly by the government, in partnership with the private sector, or via local authorities by altering their borrowing limits. The scheme could also help families to save for a deposit, with their ability to exercise Right to Buy after two years. The proceeds from any sale would then be recycled into building more low-rent, high-quality houses.

A government-backed low-rent housebuilding programme and a focus on regenerating deprived communities would leave a legacy that would genuinely make many people's lives better. It would be a great social reform that would tackle the most urgent domestic issues facing us today, improving the living standards of people currently stuck in poor-quality accommodation and ensuring that homeownership becomes the preserve of the many, not the few.

ENSURING THAT LOCAL AREAS HAVE THE HOUSING
THAT LOCAL PEOPLE WANT AND NEED

The second step for government would be supporting local areas to provide housing of the sort that local people need and that benefits the local community, rather than merely having to accept the generic design of monolithic housing developers. This would again empower local people by involving them in community-led design. It would take advantage of government- or local-authority-owned land, ideally close to town centres, with planning permission for housebuilding already provided.

A third, and potentially transformative, step would be to give local authorities the power to make innovative use of private land. This is to tackle the issue of landowners profiteering from land sales, which results in expensive, poor-quality developments that fail to meet the needs of the community. Councils should be allowed to purchase land at closer to its existing value, rather than allowing landowners to push for a speculative land value. Enabling local authorities to purchase land at reasonable prices would enable them to engage at a greater level with the local community and build the kind of development that a community wants.

Under these reforms, a council could 'zone' an area of land and invite the landowner to sell at what both sides agree is a reasonable price, with the council also having compulsory purchase powers if no agreement can be reached. Following this, the local authority could consult with the community about how the land should be used and then auction off the land to the private sector – again, based on who is best placed to meet the community's need. This is the mechanism that was used to build the new towns in the post-war period, before the law was changed in 1961 to be more generous to landowners. This would be part of a series of measures to ensure the most effective use of land, including taking steps to crack down on landbanking, with developers having to justify not building on land that they have purchased.

A RENEWED EMPHASIS ON BEAUTY IN HOUSING DESIGN

A final element of the national housebuilding programme would be a renewed emphasis on beauty and community in design. High-rise monstrosities from the 1960s, with their high-minded Corbusian intentions, weren't just aesthetically grim; they also ghettoised communities where crime and anti-social behaviour went hand in hand with the streets in the sky. The Pathfinder project, and urban regeneration projects of its ilk, continue to demonstrate the top-down approach employed by successive governments – where communities, such as those of the Welsh Streets in Liverpool, are considered dispensable and it takes Herculean efforts to reverse the decisions made in distant council chambers. The excellent work by campaigning organisations such as SAVE Britain's Heritage and Create Streets has shown that people are happier and communities more cohesive when attention is given to creating the kind of environment that people want to live in. Research has been clear that people generally want to live in streets, in houses with gardens, amidst a genuine feeling of community.

The mission to create a nation of homeowners should also include a mission to ensure that new homes are beautiful and encourage communal mixing. It has been shown across generations that the most successful forms of housing are responsive to historical context. The ambitions of Dame Henrietta Barnett at Hampstead Garden Suburb are notable, where the trust she founded catered for all classes of people and all income groups. It built a suburban landscape where roads were wide and tree-lined, houses separated by hedges (not walls), and the architectural qualities of the houses reflected the most loved aspects of vernacular architectural styles. More recently, Poundbury, which architects and metropolitan critics enjoy deriding, successfully balances both mixed use and a mixed community. In addition to its surgeries and professional offices, there is a cereal factory and a tech company making aviation components. It provides a home for literally dozens of start-ups while at the same time providing a place where people want to live, in an environment which wouldn't have been totally alien to our grandparents.

A MODERN WORKERS' CHARTER WITH THE AIM OF EMPOWERING, ENGAGING AND CAPITALISING WORKERS

British workers are some of the least engaged and most overworked employees in Europe. There is little attempt to engage them in decision-making, especially when compared with northern European examples of workplace cooperation. It is particularly ironic that the model of employee engagement that exists in Germany, with worker representatives on boards, was one insisted upon by the British government following the war. It was also a model proposed by the Bullock Report in the late 1970s, which was at that time rejected by a trade union movement that had already descended into the idiocy of hard-left militancy.

British workers are also among the worst impacted by the disparity between capital and wages that was highlighted by Thomas Piketty in his recent blockbuster *Capital in the Twenty-First Century*. Despite the goal of creating a share-owning democracy, the proportion of private individuals owning shares actually decreased following the privatisations of the 1980s. Only 11 per cent of shares in UK-traded companies are owned by individuals – a proportion that has almost halved in recent decades – and too few companies provide share equity to their workers. The fall in share and homeownership means that the rhetoric of popular capitalism hasn't come close to being matched by reality, contributing to a sense that rising prosperity was something that was happening to other people.

At the same time as this decline in share and property ownership, wages have hit a prolonged period of stagnation, meaning that capital has been far outperforming wages. This was notably the case in those organisations that saw executive pay grow in a way that had little relevance to performance, with those executives also benefiting from substantial share options.

Changing the nature of the British firm would make our economy more productive, and our employees more engaged. As well as reforming the nature of the firm in a way that engages and capitalises workers, it's also crucial to consider how all can work with dignity and security.

The Brexit process does provide opportunities, but it also comes with risks. Although imperfect, the Social Chapter does, at least, lay down a minimum of workers' rights. It's also true that the least imaginative of the laissez-faire Brexiteers view any kind of workers' right as an unnecessary regulation on business and an incursion on the proper workings of the free market. As set out earlier, such a view is utopian nonsense and workers should not be exploited on the whim of a free market utopia, much as workers shouldn't be sacrificed to benefit a left-wing utopia.

The beginning of a Workers' Charter should be to set in stone *at least* the same level of workers' rights as contained in the Social Chapter. A brave government could, and should, go further, including in the charter a bold commitment to enshrining workers' rights in law, but also laying the framework for a new era of cooperation and prosperity.

Employee engagement within the firm should be the norm, rather than the exception. The successful economies discussed earlier, who place a premium on skills, also tend to place a premium on proper management–worker cooperation within the firm. To achieve this, having worker representation at every level, including on the board and the remuneration committee, is important. What is more important, however, is entrenching a culture of engagement and cooperation throughout the firm.

This belief in a shared success has dissipated at a time when capital has diverged so comprehensively from wages. Since the banking crash, the FTSE 100 has risen by 59 per cent and wages have barely risen at all.

This means that shareholders within a firm, generally those who are managers and executives, are feeling more of a company's success than those members of the workforce not impacted by its share price. Clearly, corporate success is not being shared within a company, leading to the more general sense of fragmentation within society and the economy. This hits low-paid workers particularly hard, as they don't see the benefits of their hard work, are often forced to work anti-social hours at short notice, and have less flexibility to see their families or play active roles in their communities.

This low pay is also more likely to impact people based in and around England's forgotten towns. Research by the Resolution Foundation has found that 24 per cent of workers in the Tees Valley are considered to be low paid, with the figure being 24 per cent in Sheffield, 23 per cent in North Yorkshire and 21 per cent in Newcastle. By contrast, low pay only accounts for one tenth of jobs in London. It also finds that towns have far greater problems with low pay than cities within 'city regions'. For example, one in seven of those working in Manchester and Trafford are low paid, compared to one in four in outlying areas, such as Rochdale, Wigan and Bury.

There are a number of ways in which this situation should be rectified. First, minimum standards should be entrenched within the charter. This doesn't just mean meeting the Social Chapter level, it also means taking steps to tackle the insecure work culture. For example, there should be severe restrictions on the ability of firms to impose insecure, short notice on workers.

The Charter would also encourage firms to offer an ownership structure that goes beyond the proposals unveiled by John McDonnell, which acknowledge the problem, but amount to double taxing and severely limit the number of shares that firms can provide to their workers. Instead, firms would be expected to report annually on the proportion of their workforce who were empowered with share ownership. They would also be expected to explain why this didn't apply to all levels within the firm. Companies with fewer than 10,000 employees should also be incentivised through the tax system to provide share ownership to their workers.

A final step to further empower workers is to encourage and maintain mutualisation. This represents a way of both ensuring that public services are more directly embedded in the community and giving staff a real say in how the company is run. David Cameron and Nick Clegg both committed to measures to extend mutualisation when they took power, but the reality failed to match the rhetoric. Mutuals must form part of the new economic and political settlement. There should be a drive for mutualisation as part of the broad devolution settlement and the mutual model can also be used as way of boosting measures to renew town centres.

TAX CUTS TO BENEFIT WORKING PEOPLE

As we've noted throughout this book, recent decades and, in particular, the years since the banking crash have seen workers not sharing in the benefits of 'growth'. Growth itself has been anaemic, but most of its benefits have been felt by some owners of capital and the already wealthy. The goal of politics and economics, as I've proposed, must be to set out and deliver a range of policies to benefit the majority and, in particular, those who have been left behind in recent decades.

This will partially be done, as previously explained, by broadening access to capital and ensuring that workers and not just bosses are able to benefit from share ownership schemes within companies. However, there are other policy levers that can be used to ensure that the majority share more of the wealth they create.

The first, of course, is through the tax system. The idea to increase the starting rate of tax to £10,000, and gradually increasing above that, was a very important way of using fiscal policy to help the disadvantaged and it lifted millions of the poorest out of tax altogether. Its impact as a fiscal tool since then has been reduced. Any increase in the tax-free allowance will now, by its very nature, not impact the poorest (who have already been taken out of tax), but be felt by all taxpayers equally.

This should be tackled in four ways. First, any income tax cuts should be targeted at those on low and middle incomes. So, the government should look to deliver an income tax cut for those on less than £50,000 a year, and this cut could be greater for those on less than £35,000 a year so that the benefits are felt the most by the lowest paid.

Second, the government should look to enable workers to take home more through the benefit system. Universal Credit is by no means a perfect model. Nevertheless, after years of implementation, it would be expensive folly to seek to overturn it now. Instead, the taper (the amount by which someone's benefit reduces when they go into work) should be reduced considerably.

Third, the government should end the freeze on in-work

TAKING BACK CONTROL

benefits. This might have been necessary during the period of austerity, but is now worsening the divide between forgotten towns, where low pay predominates, and the rest of the country. It has made life more difficult for those who are struggling to get by in low-paid work. Over the long term, investment in skills, good jobs and housing will, of course, help to improve the situation. In the short term, however, ending the freeze on in-work benefits will make a genuine difference to people's lives.

Finally, government should increase the National Insurance threshold from its present rate of £8,424 to at least £10,000, with a goal of matching the Income Tax threshold (currently £12,500) as soon as possible. Over the coming years, government should prioritise increasing the National Insurance threshold rather than the Income Tax threshold. This would disproportionately benefit those on low incomes.

A PAY RISE FOR WORKERS

The state, however, shouldn't take on all of the burden for ensuring that workers share the benefits of growth. Business also has a role to play in making sure that workers are given a fair share of profits and that these genuine 'wealth creators' get a share in the benefits of corporate success.

A report by Profit Watch UK showed that between July and September 2018, the top 350 companies in the UK set a quarterly profit record, posting a total of £218 billion over the three-month period. The disparity between executive pay and worker pay has

271

also become more marked. The FTSE 100 median pay increased by 11 per cent for CEOs between 2016 and 2017 to £3.93 million, and the mean increased by some 23 per cent to £5.66 million, whereas the median wage in the UK was around £27,000. The CIPD found that the mean ratio between CEO salaries and the average pay of company workers was 145:1.

Two important public policy moves in recent decades have helped to improve the situation for British workers. Despite laissez-faire warnings of millions of job losses, the introduction of the national minimum wage in 1998 actually had little or no impact on unemployment. Cases of people being paid a pound an hour disappeared and there was no deleterious impact on jobs. Indeed, there is strong evidence that the growth in wages and motivation led to a rise in productivity in the economy as people felt more valued in their jobs. It all but eliminated the scourge of poverty pay.

The introduction of the national living wage in 2016 is something that I campaigned vigorously for, again faced with siren warnings from hardcore laissez-faire activists. Again, it has proven to be a substantial public policy success, with the Resolution Foundation arguing that the policy has caused the 'fastest fall in low pay for forty years'. George Osborne should be congratulated for the political bravery in introducing such a policy – a valuable example of when he was prepared to genuinely embrace the One Nation tradition (Macmillan proposed a minimum wage in *The Middle Way*). Both of these public policy successes show that there is room for further progress in helping workers to see the fruits of their labour.

There's scope to build even further on the success of this policy. The national living wage of £7.83 is still short of the £9 level (£10.55 in London) set as part of the voluntary living wage, which is set by an independent panel of academics and experts based on what people genuinely need to get by. Only thirty-nine companies in the FTSE 100 are signed up to the voluntary living wage.

The Workers' Charter would set the national living wage as a bare minimum but would also state that businesses with more than 1,000 employees should publish a charter report annually, showing steps that they are taking to tackle low pay and to advance towards paying the voluntary living wage. This submission should also set out the ratio between the CEO's salary and the pay of the lowest paid person in the company.

Evidence from recent years and the evidence that paying the living wage increases worker morale and corporate performance means that government could legislate on this topic. To build on the success of the national living wage, government should legislate that companies with over 20,000 employees should pay the 'real' living wage and that other companies should look towards paying it.

RENEWING LITTLE PLATOONS

Throughout this book, I've discussed how the bonds that tie us together have become frayed in recent decades as our society has become more atomised and less cohesive. This has been most notable in the town of Consett and others like it, which have suffered from the demise of heavy industry and the inability to create new jobs that had both the dignity and worth of the old ones.

The 'little platoons' that were once the backbone of the country and these communities continue to be hugely important, but they must also be re-energised and renewed. Strengthening communities must form a part of the new political and economic settlement that people clearly called for in the 2016 referendum.

Recreating One Nation should be the goal of this settlement, which would give towns like Consett and Barnsley as preeminent a place in public life and economic discourse as the City of London. Prosperity hubs, focused on those towns that have been most substantially 'left behind' by deindustrialisation, should be at the core of a nationwide package of reindustrialisation, skills training, worker empowerment and community revival.

At the centre of all of these proposals is a desire to give agency and control to individuals and to build an environment in which the private sector and entrepreneurs can thrive. Renewing One Nation would pay political dividends to a political party that enthusiastically embraced, and implemented, this agenda. That, however, would be a positive side effect. The most important result of a renewed One Nation agenda would be to improve the lives of people who have long been forgotten.

ACKNOWLEDGEMENTS

Thank you to my parents, George and Lynda, for their constant support and encouragement.

Huge thanks to all those who have offered thoughts, guidance and review.

Thanks to Ben Furnival, Jim Curry, Simon Cawte, Craig Barnett, Joan Barnett, Steve Akehurst, Tom Mauchline, Andy Laird, James Probert, Luke Maynard, Rosie Luff, Jesse Norman, Neil O'Brien, Nick Faith, Anthony McDonald, Tim Shipman, Jason Cowley, Naomi Gummer, Katie O'Donovan and Nicklas Lundblad, among others.

Particular appreciation to Olivia Beattie and the team at Biteback for putting their faith in this project.

ABOUT THE AUTHOR

DAVID SKELTON has been a highly influential figure in politics, policy development and public service reform for over a decade. He was head of research at Policy Exchange between 2011 and 2013 and went on to found Renewal, with the aim of broadening the appeal of the Conservative Party and pushing the policy concerns of the 'left-behind'.

Tim Shipman in the *Sunday Times* has described Skelton as 'one of the three most important thinkers on the right' and George Eaton in the *New Statesman* has described him as the 'thinker that Tories should listen to'. ConservativeHome described him as '*the* Tory who understands the North', while Renewal was described by *The Economist* as a potential 'brains trust' of the modern Tory Party and by *The Times* as 'tearing up the definitions of left and right'.

Skelton's ideas about reforming Toryism have also been acknowledged as being particularly powerful by many on the left, who fear the power of his proposals to redraw the political map. LabourList described Skelton as 'the Tory who Labour should be afraid of'. The then Labour leader Ed Miliband spoke of Skelton as 'one of the few Tories who understands and cares about inequality'.

Owen Jones said that the left should be fearful of Skelton's attempt to create a Toryism that 'relates to people's everyday issues and concerns'. Mary Riddell, in the *Telegraph*, said that Skelton's ideas being adopted by the Tories would 'prove lethal to Labour's chances' and that this would mutate into 'terror [among Labour leaders] if they caught on in Downing Street'.

David has written regularly for a number of publications, including *The Guardian*, *New Statesman*, the *Daily Telegraph*, Prospect, ConservativeHome and *The Spectator*, as well as appearing regularly on BBC Radio and TV, ITN and Sky News.

INDEX